Dialogues on Power and Space

Dialogues on Power and Space

Carl Schmitt

Edited by Andreas Kalyvas and Federico Finchelstein

Translated with an introduction and notes by
Samuel Garrett Zeitlin

polity

First published in German as *Gespräch über die Macht und den Zugang zum Machthaber*, © Klett-Cotta – J.G. Cotta'sche Buchhandlung Nachfolger GmbH, Stuttgart, 1954/2008, and *Gespräch über den Neuen Raum*, © Duncker & Humblot GmbH, Berlin, 1958/1995
This English edition © Polity Press, 2015

Polity Press
65 Bridge Street
Cambridge CB2 1UR, UK

Polity Press
350 Main Street
Malden, MA 02148, USA

ISBN-13: 978-0-7456-8868-8 (hardback)
ISBN-13: 978-0-7456-8869-5 (paperback)

A catalogue record for this book is available from the British Library.

Library of Congress Cataloging-in-Publication Data

Schmitt, Carl, 1888-1985.
  [Gesprach Uber die Macht und den Zugang zum Machthaber und Gesprach Uber den neuen Raum. English]
  Dialogues on power and space / Carl Schmitt.
    pages cm
  Includes bibliographical references and index.
  ISBN 978-0-7456-8868-8 (hardback) -- ISBN 978-0-7456-8869-5 (pbk.) 1.
Power (Social sciences) I. Title.
  JC330.S24 2015
  303.3--dc23

                                                    2015004926

Typeset in 11 on 14 pt Adobe Caslon by
Servis Filmsetting Ltd, Stockport, Cheshire

For further information on Polity, visit our website:politybooks.com

Contents

Translator's Introduction

The translations in this volume are based on the texts of Carl Schmitt's *Gespräche* established by Gerd Giesler on the basis of comparing the 1954 and 1958 printed versions with the marginalia, annotations, and editorial changes found in Schmitt's personal copies of each of the works in the Schmitt *Nachlass*. In each case, the most recent version published by Gerd Giesler served as the source of the translation. In the case of Schmitt's *Gespräch über die Macht und den Zugang zum Machthaber* [Dialogue on Power and Access to the Holder of Power], this was the 2008 edition published by Klett-Cotta with an afterword by Giesler. In the case of Schmitt's *Gespräch über den Neuen Raum* [Dialogue on New Space], this was the 1994 Akademie Verlag edition of the *Gespräche* prepared by Gerd Giesler. In translating both dialogues, the texts were compared with the 1954 and 1958 editions of the works in question, as well as with the 1962 Spanish translation prepared by Schmitt's daughter and only child, Anima Schmitt de Otero. Some observed differences and variants between the various editions are noted in the translator's notes to this edition. In addition, the notes and references have benefited from an examination of Giovanni

Gurisatti's apparatus to his 2012 Italian translation of the *Dialogues* [Carl Schmitt, *Dialogo sul potere*, ed. Giovanni Gurisatti (Milano: Adelphi Edizioni, 2012)] as well as from the notes and apparatus to Günter Maschke's 1995 German edition of the *Dialogue on New Space* (which prints the 1958 version of the text) included in *Staat, Großraum, Nomos. Arbeiten aus den Jahren 1916–1969* (Berlin: Duncker & Humblot, 1995).

The work aims to provide an accurate translation of Schmitt's German within the limits of readable English, while preserving something of the tenor and tone of the dialogue form as Schmitt deploys it. To this end, contractions were occasionally deployed in the English to maintain something of the informality, sharpness, and speed of the *Dialogues*. However, technical terms in Schmitt's political vocabulary such as constitution [*Verfassung*], state [*Staat*], power [*Macht*], and space [*Raum*] have been rendered consistently throughout the translations to allow English readers to track and interpret Schmitt's concepts, terminology, and usage.

One such term, meriting sensitive and consistent treatment, is "the human" [*der Mensch*] which is used by Schmitt's characters with some frequency throughout both dialogues. It is not clear, for a variety of reasons, that Schmitt understands his notion of "the human" [*der Mensch*] to cover all that a contemporary reader might understand to be pertinent to the species *Homo sapiens*. For reasons of philological and historical accuracy, in order to allow English readers to interpret Schmitt's notion of "the human" and to make both his political vocabulary as well as his political anthropology accessible to an English readership, *der Mensch* and its equivalents have been rendered as "the human" or "human" throughout both translations.

Translator's Acknowledgments

For helpful readings, assistance, and corrections of earlier versions of these translations, I am thankful to Ron Hassner, Kinch Hoekstra, Tobias Hurth, Victoria Kahn, Elliott Karstadt, Sarah Lambert, Pierre-Yves Modicom, Andreas Peter, David Ragazzoni, George Schwab, Shannon Stimson, Felix Waldmann, Joanna Williamson, and the anonymous reviewers for Polity.

I am thankful to Professor George D. Schwab for generously granting approval of these translations.

I have been very fortunate to have had many great teachers: Mark Bevir, Annabel Brett, Chris Brooke, Wendy Brown, Timothy Hampton, Robert Hass, Ron Hassner, Sudhir Hazareesingh, Kinch Hoekstra, Victoria Kahn, Noel Malcolm, Heinrich Meier, Stephen Mulhall, Diego Pirillo, John Robertson, Richard Serjeantson, Ethan Shagan, Shannon Stimson, Adam Swift, and Steve Weber. To Kinch Hoekstra and Shannon Stimson, I am especially grateful as teachers and mentors, for the privilege and delight of studying political philosophy and the history of political thought with them at Berkeley, during what have been, for me, the happiest of times.

I am thankful for the love of my family – my mother, Elizabeth, my sister, Ellie, and my dear friend and companion, Joanna.

The work of this translation is dedicated to Professors Victoria Kahn and Shannon C. Stimson, with gratitude for their teaching and intellectual generosity and with admiration for their scholarship.

Samuel Garrett Zeitlin

Editors' Introduction

Andreas Kalyvas[1] and Federico Finchelstein

In the early 1950s, Carl Schmitt, one of the most controversial and influential political thinkers and jurists of the twentieth century, offered to the Hesse public radio [*Hessischer Rundfunk*] a script for a dialogue on power and access to the holder of power. The result was the *Dialogue on Power and Access to the Holder of Power*. Interestingly, he presented it as a conversation between himself, "C.S.," and a youth, "Y." First performed by German actors with the title "Principles of Power," it was then published as a small book in German and as an article in Spanish by the end of 1954. Then in 1958, Schmitt published another dialogue on the related subject of space and politics, *Dialogue on New Space*. This text is a discussion between an historian, a hard scientist, and a "North American" called "MacFuture."[2] In 1962 both dialogues appeared together in Spain as a single book entitled *Diálogos,* translated by his daughter Anima, for which Schmitt wrote a special introduction.[3] In 1994 both dialogues appeared in a German edition.[4] Now for the first time these two dialogues along with the Spanish prologue are finally published in English.

The two texts were born out of the period when Schmitt,

after having been imprisoned for his Nazi activities during the war, had retreated to an unchartered intellectual space outside of the university. His early cold-war experience was one of pessimist introspection, far away from the trenches of his earlier political engagements, defined by his self-understanding as a "powerless" person.[5] This retreat, however, had nothing to do with silence. On the contrary, he considered himself to be in a position similar to Machiavelli's self-exile.[6] His projective identification with Machiavelli was not uncharacteristic of this period in his life, when he was trying to make sense of his personal fate as well as the new post-Second World War geopolitical order. He reformulated the canon for a time when he was no longer explicitly involved in a political project. As he had done with Thomas Hobbes and Juan Donoso Cortés, especially before the war, Schmitt staged his intellectual predicament on canonical figures of political thought writing in moments of intense crisis, world historical transformations, and political failures. For instance, while in prison he had framed the start of his postwar work in relation to the intellectual fate of another thinker concerned with the sweeping transformations of European politics during the previous century: Alexis de Tocqueville.[7] This comparison implies that, like Tocqueville and also, before him, Machiavelli, Schmitt was equally defeated and faced his own defeat. But this defeat ironically meant that he was liberated by the constraints of domestic politics, from which he had already started to distance himself by the end of the Nazi period, following his public denunciation by the SS but still under the protection of prominent Nazi leaders such as Hans Frank and Hermann Göring, hence turning his attention almost exclusively to geopolitics, international law, and global politics.

Interestingly, this also was a period when some of his most important works found a receptive audience, mainly in small private circles in Germany but perhaps more importantly in Iberian and Latin American academic contexts. One could argue that this was an intellectual displacement for Schmitt. To be sure, he had already established deep connections with Spanish-speaking audiences before the war. However, these relations were further developed and cultivated after formal academic channels were foreclosed to him in Germany and Western Europe. Thus, in this postwar context his work found a public haven among the remaining European dictatorships and the newly emerging populisms of Latin America. He was a constant visitor to Franco's Spain where he delivered key lectures.[8] For a time, he also seriously considered emigrating to General Juan Peron's Argentina.[9] These contexts were to provide him with a unique and privileged public opening to his more specific and vast academic writings. To be sure, Schmitt never abandoned the academy altogether. Especially in Franco's Spain, but also in Argentina and other Latin American countries, he found a very welcoming academic audience. But in Germany, due to his Nazi past and his refusal to de-Nazify, Schmitt was barred from a formal University position. He clearly resented this. During the 1950s, Schmitt frequently complained in private about what he saw as the constant humiliations and the ceaseless venomous polemics of postwar Germany. As a former Nazi, Schmitt saw himself as a victim of alien invaders. From then on, he almost never addressed his fascist past in public nor did he make frequent public reference to the regime's conception, planning and extermination of millions of European Jews. Although during this period he critically assessed Hitler, he also occasionally expressed in private his antisemitic prejudices on the "Jewish spirit" and insisted that the "assimilated Jew is the new enemy." He also privately expressed to friends how he regarded the legitimacy of the German Federal Republic in dubious terms. He constructed a myth of himself as the victim of his times even comparing his postwar experiences with those of the Jews under National Socialism. Schmitt found it hard to live in a new democratic Germany while at the same he applied his thinking to question the more abstract theoretical roots of its liberal foundations. Tellingly, he conceived his own trajectory as a stealth epic of sub-maritime nature. He saw it as an apocalyptic odyssey in the dark: "Like a U-boat that continually rebuilds itself, I continue on my submarine, subterranean, sub-lunar voyage through fire and water."[10]

The two *Dialogues* showcase his underground ambition to remain a public intellectual, against what he perceived as a deliberate attempt to silence those who had been associated with the Third Reich. For instance, when the first dialogue, on power, was published it stirred considerable consternation and controversy among anti-fascists who had resisted the public presence of former Nazi intellectuals such as Schmitt. The German magazine *Die Zeit* initially published an abridged version of this dialogue and a rather positive presentation of the author that led to renunciations, resignations, and firing.[11] However, at that time, as has often been the case with Schmitt after 1945, the controversy was related to Schmitt's Nazi past rather than to the nature of the arguments made in the *Dialogue on Power*. All in all, after the controversies faded, the text was somehow lost in the midst of other works by Schmitt. The same happened to the subsequent *Dialogue on New Space*. And yet, both dialogues, are of key importance when situated within Schmitt's vast *oeuvre*.

I

What is striking in these two texts is the form of argumentation and the dialogical genre that Schmitt chooses to adopt. Furthermore, in the first dialogue on power he appears as one of the interlocutors, as the subject who knows. In this self-assigned role, he educates the youth. In the second dialogue, on space, the voice of knowledge is impersonated by "a certain type of historian, somewhat antiquated, but solid, in his seventies" who is engaged, "in a pacific and prolix" conversation with a positivist scientist in his fifties.[12] Thus, while the first dialogue showcases Schmitt as a protagonist, the second on new spaces ventriloquizes Schmitt's teachings, which conduct the discussion. This second dialogue replicates the first in that he assigns to the historian a role almost identical to that of himself (C.S.) in the first dialogue. But as opposed to the first dialogue between two speakers, the second setting is disrupted by a third participant, "a young North American," who "crashes" into the conversation.[13]

One might argue that the pedagogical intention of the dialogues replaces the loss of the classroom experience that Schmitt suffered after the war. Tellingly, mass media function as a substitute for the lost intimacy of the seminar model whereby the audience is transformed into his students. Both dialogues seem to belong to a longstanding tradition of works from Plato to Sigmund Freud, although Schmitt claimed that the narrative of the book was far from Plato: "This is not a dialogue in the style of Plato. The student is no

Alcibiades, and neither is the old man a Socrates. He guards himself well from having metaphysical constructions. "[14] For Schmitt, the two dialogues are not about the philosophical quest for justice but instead they focus on the "descriptive unfolding of the dialectic immanent in each power."[15]

The form and style of the two dialogues share some common elements. First of all, it is worth noting that Schmitt constructed two rather unsophisticated and inexperienced interlocutors, somehow stereotypical figures, whom he presented as "the youth" and "the North American."[16] Moreover, one could argue that in their peculiar style, the Schmittian dialogues show affinities with Freud's *The Future of an Illusion*. Both texts are highly pessimistic and present the author as an agent of analytic illumination through the means of dialogic engagement. But in a sense, they do not demonstrate a real dialogue, an open-ended conversation among equals. Rather, both Schmitt's dialogues confront naive persons versus the subject who is supposed to know. Ignorance and knowledge face each other. However, if in Freud knowledge is related to unmaking and framing the structural mythical conditions of the mind, in Schmitt it is closely tied to the pessimistic nature of his postwar historicism, a gloomy philosophy of history. Furthermore, the Schmittian dialogues are reminiscent, in text and form, of the Catholic education manuals that were typical of the 1920s and 1930s. They might even be seen as a kind of theoretical catechesis on power and space, whereby truth is firmly rooted in the answers. In fact, the two dialogues on power and space begin with a theological thrust. Tellingly, Schmitt later described the second conversation as having "theological" dimensions while the first is launched with a short excursus on the problem of the divine origins of power. However, this truth consists of a secular and immanent understanding of power, place, and politics, or as he put it, "The human is a human to the human" and "the son of the firmly grounded earth." Hence Schmitt's postwar humanist 'turn.'[17]

II

In the first dialogue, the question of power is addressed in relation to its pre-modern formulations, which Schmitt mainly identifies with the biblical tradition of divine origins. This is a tradition, he argues, that modernity has rejected in favor of a humanist understanding according to which power is created and exercised only by humans over other humans. So, in this text, Schmitt revisits his earlier thesis on political theology as the secularization of theological concepts by introducing now the idea of "humanization."[18] Political modernity is defined by the humanization of power, which coincides with the collapse of ultimate grounds and a widespread recognition of the immanent sources of authority. The historicity of power is a central element in Schmitt. Power is rooted in historical human subjectivity and is intrinsic to human relations. "The power that one man exerts over other men originates from men themselves," he asserts.

Respectively, Schmitt reaffirms the concept of political power as "power over," which emphasizes the hierarchical relationship of domination between rulers and ruled, the command and obedience nexus, and the desire for protection, only to show how the superiority and autonomy of power is dialectically caught up with its own impotence and weakness. He describes this relationship as the internal "dialectic of self-assertion and self-alienation," which no human power can escape and that defines the fundamental attribute of politics.[19] He highlights the autonomy of power even with respect to the powerful. He explicitly focuses on the issue of the limits of the powerful vis-à-vis power by directing attention to the limits of power as performed by the powerful. To be sure, these two spheres are not mutually exclusive, and perhaps this is even a question of implicit emphasis in the dialogue. But Schmitt stresses the relationship between power and the "antechamber of power" as a way to understand this "dialectic of self-affirmation and self-alienation," which defines the relationship between the powerful and power.[20] In short, he shows how the autonomy of power leads to a tension between the affirmation of power and the isolation of the powerful. It is a tension that reveals that the inner dialectic of power works also as an informal limitation on the holder of power that precludes the fusion of the powerful with power. This dialectic becomes the object of the dialogue, which then can be interpreted as an attempt to understand the dialectical nature of human power, that is, a power purely immanent, lacking theological and naturalistic extra-social foundations.

But the dialogue is more than a mere description of power. It also consists of a critique. Schmitt's post-foundationalism does not solely speak of a politics after the demise of ultimate transcendent grounds. It also takes the form of a warning that seeks to expose the contemporary predicament of power. The unprecedented technological innovations of the last century have transformed politics to such a degree that for the first time in human history power has become "undialectical," that is, it has superseded the internal dialectic between itself and impotence. A gap between power and powerlessness separating the two has come to replace the inner dialectic of power and impotence. Contemporary power is freed from any weakness. This reality of power, Schmitt claims, exceeds the reality of the humans. The new technologies of the twentieth century are dehumanizing power, calling into question the very possibility of politics in a motorized age where the human is being displaced by *technè*.[21]

Schmitt's dialogue on power is foremost a critique of "late" modernity. The self-assertion of modern power that avoids the opposite movement of self-alienation marks a momentous break in the historical evolution of power. The singularity of modern power consists in its ability to assert itself without any alienation, having eliminated the internal presence of powerlessness. It is a non-alienated power, without traces of impotence left, and thus released from the inner constraints of a dialectical logic. In this way, Schmitt asserted, power has become hubristic, an excess driven by the totalizing tendencies of an absolute unity. By overcoming the inner tension of power, modernity has also abandoned all informal checks and intrinsic impediments that in the past had prevented power from achieving total closure.

The dialogue is a conversation between a moralist form of thinking, which Schmitt equated with naiveté in politics, with his own dialectical thought that highlighted the absolute historicity of power through its current undialectical transformation.[22] The youth, "Y", presents a moral framework for thinking power, whereas as "C.S.", Schmitt prefers to emphasize the dialectical tensions rooted in power and the pernicious consequences of any final resolution. Tellingly, Schmitt announces this critique of modern power by stating his own lack of power. From this absence – the lack of power in his own person, which one could also present as an actual historical loss[23] – he concludes that his own position is somewhat neutral in that as an analyst he is focused on the "contemplation and description" of historical phenomena. This dialogue then is Schmitt's explicit attempt to grasp what he saw as the inherent logic of all power.

As a critique of modern power, the first dialogue also renews some links with Schmitt's Weimar writings and anticipates his somber and pessimistic postwar observations on war, law, enmity, violence, and transnational politics. Although the *Dialogue on Power* can also be read as a continuation of his dialogues on Nazi power with the interrogators from Nuremberg, where Schmitt disingenuously adopted a much more critical view of the role of the leader in fascism, there are also significant differences in meaning and context between these dialogues. At Nuremberg, Schmitt presented his own involvement in Nazism as a result of his desire to "give the term National Socialism my own meaning." In addition to defining himself as an "intellectual adventurer" Schmitt recommended to his interrogators that his "writings should not be judged until they have been thoroughly studied in their scientific context." In this context, he reflected on the notion of Nazi power as the forger of a new historical form of "total dictatorship." He also advanced a first version of the access to power in that dictatorial context that he also called a "totalitarian state."[24] Clearly, the Nuremberg dialogues on Nazism were not an ideal setting for Schmitt; as an accused man, he was legally and conceptually restrained. In contrast, the *Dialogue*'s fictional setting allows Schmitt to reflect on power without the constraints of the postwar context and his own role in the period that had preceded it. In this imaginary landscape, a play on power, where the subject position of the author was not put in question but it rather became the starting point of the arguments, the

Dialogue allows Schmitt the opportunity to provide his most systematic treatment of the question of power.

Respectively, without the constraints imposed by domestic and personal histories, Schmitt leaves behind his analysis of dictatorship. More importantly, and perhaps for the first time, he embraces an articulate critical view of the political role of leadership. Thus, the *Dialogue* presents a cold-war bridge between the writings of his fascist years and his subsequent disillusionment with the powerful as well as a deeper and more complex understanding of the paradoxes and risks of power as such.

III

If the first dialogue on power ends with a warning about modernity, the second dialogue on space concludes with the hopeful wish that the political impasses of modernity associated with unencumbered technology will find a resolution when humanity returns back to the land to reaffirm a territorial existence. In other words, the problem of power unbounded by any dialectical necessity that Schmitt discussed in the first dialogue can only be resolved spatially, that is, through a global reorganization of world politics, as envisioned in the second dialogue.

This second dialogue, like the first, begins with the Bible, where God creates the world through "a succession of several separations."[25] These are three constitutive distinctions between light and darkness, heaven and earth, and land and sea. It is the last distinction that concerns Schmitt the most in his attempt to reaffirm the primacy of territorial existence as the only living-space [*Lebensraum*] for humans: Behemoth against Leviathan.

Schmitt had initially defended the primacy of the land over the sea during the war years and now he evokes it again in the context of the cold war by proposing a geo-political reading of the Bible that emphasizes the institution of primordial spatial categories and their antagonistic relationships. Here the notion of a living-space first appears in a theological and mythical fashion only to be obliquely transformed into a (trans-) historical theory of world-history as the perennial conflict between land and sea.

On this level, the dialogue clearly mirrors Schmitt's central concern with the United States and the Soviet Union as the two poles of the cold war. MacFuture, who crashes into the discussion in the dialogue, uninvited, presents his objections to the historian from a confident North American perspective. He extols the rise of a novel era where power, technology, and space will be literally put in the realm of the cosmic. A new geo-political history will begin in ways similar to the age of the colonial expansion of Europe. MacFuture is sort of a prophet of a technological and nuclear reorganization of political space. For him, the new spaces are related to the cold-war era where the United States presents itself as opening political spaces beyond the terrestrial. The historian refutes this idea that, as he nonetheless recognizes, challenges his geopolitical scheme of land and sea. For Schmitt, the colonization of space does not inaugurate a new realm for the political but rather it reproduces existing and exhausted modalities of power and space.[26]

This dialogue equally can be read along with the *Nomos of the Earth* (1950) and also with the mythical approach in *Hamlet or Hecuba* (1956). Actually the *Dialogue* straddles the conceptual boundaries between the *Nomos*, his *Hamlet* and the *Theory of the Partisan* (1963) and the very different

Nazi context of his writings on *Land and Sea* (1942) and international law (1933–45).[27] The contextual, the transcendental, and the political are mutually embedded. However, the transcendental thrust of his political theology is not as relevant in the *Dialogues* as it is in the theory of *Nomos* and the *Partisan*. During this period, Schmitt stressed the constant secularizing tendencies of the geo-political dimensions of power, its "humanization." He spoke of a break with the medieval doctrine of just war around the sixteenth century and the concomitant theologization of the enemy by way of the absolute category of evil.

This break with the theological, codified in the Westphalian Eurocentric order, was challenged by England's rise to world prominence. With the arrival of the first global maritime empire in the eighteenth century, a historical change occurred, a "global spatial revolution," which included the industrial revolution, intimately associated with the age of conquests and the new global consciousness, and the universal ambitions of liberalism and, later on, communism.[28] All these changes ushered in a new era, both historically and normatively, as they became constitutive of disorder, instability, and anomie.[29] The *Dialogue on New Space* represents a central key to understand Schmitt's re-orientation toward a global political theory, permeated by a reluctant but evident normative orientation, fixed on the ideas of human stability and security, presented in the form of Hobbesian realism, which he began to develop during the early years of the cold war. It also suggests a concerted effort to understand the new spatial organization of a bipolar world and how the elements of air and outer space have disrupted the historical antithesis between land and sea by opening up novel spaces that could radically alter the contours of inherited politics.[30]

Much as in the first dialogue, Schmitt articulates a critical theory of global politics that was ushered by the British Empire, capitalism, industrial revolution, and the technological innovations it brought into being, especially in relation to war-making. For Schmitt, the main spatial transformation that the twentieth century experienced was the end of the antithesis between land and sea and the emergence of new universal spatiality that threatens the very existence of the planet Earth as such. While in the first dialogue Schmitt traced the exhaustion of the inner dialectic of power, in the second, he focused on the collapse of the land–sea opposition. In both cases, however, the consequences were the same: the formation of a boundless, spaceless power, detached from its inner and geographical determinations, absolute, indeterminate, in constant, ceaseless motion. It is a de-territorialized power, Schmitt warned, that could potentially obliterate the human.

IV

The two dialogues bridge the political and theoretical trajectory of Carl Schmitt. And they do so in a way that combines Schmitt's own explicit desire of reaching the widest possible public – in fact this is probably the least technical and the most public-sphere-oriented work by Schmitt – with the historical and theoretical attempt to reframe his work for the postwar world. This is a period that is often associated with the moment when Schmitt decided to retreat to the relative silence of the non-academic world as he had promised to his allied interrogators in Nuremberg. In other words, he was to write and think from the privacy of the home. If he intended to engage in this sort of internal exile, the two

Dialogues are a rather curious way to achieve this. He did so by engaging in a public explanation of his theory of power in the then most popular form of communication: radio.[31] The idea was to provide a public opening to his more specific and vast academic writings. To be sure, Schmitt, never abandoned the academy altogether. Especially in Franco's Spain, but also in Argentina and other Latin American countries, he found a very receptive audience. But in Germany, due to his refusal to de-Nazify he never formally returned to an academic position.

The *Dialogues* show his somewhat failed attempt to become a public intellectual after 1945, despite what he rightly perceived as an attempt to downplay the intellectual prominence of those who had been associated with fascism. In fact, Schmitt's Nazi past over-determined the reception of the two dialogues but the arguments were generally ignored. The two texts were somehow lost in the midst of other more specialized works by Schmitt. And yet, their key importance is obvious when considering his critical philosophy of the history of power and space as presented in this book.

Dialogues on Power and Space

Carl Schmitt

Prologue to the 1962 Spanish Edition[1]

Archimedes of Syracuse, the celebrated master of ancient technology, took it upon himself to move the universe if you gave him a resting point. The modern Archimedes acts in a distinct manner. The physicists and technologists of today penetrate into the cosmos without seeking or asking for any resting point. They are opening immeasurable new spaces, and are transcending all the measures and dimensions of the earth and of the human itself.

In spite of this, however, they are not without a resting point. They are in the service of determined political powers, especially the United States of America and the Soviet Union. The career of modern physicists, technologists, and cosmonauts is determined by the question of who shall rule the immeasurable new spaces. This is, in sum, a pure problem of power. Up until the present, the astounding discoveries and inventions of the modern Archimedes have principally served to solve problems of political power.

But with this we turn back in repentance from the immeasurable spaces of the cosmos to our little earth. Here below the new spaces and the new holders of power will be decided upon.[2]

It is thus concerning space and power. These are also the themes of our dialogues. They redirect our attention away from these fantastic visions back towards our planet. In the first dialogue,[3] a certain type of historian, somewhat antiquated, but solid, in his seventies, talks with a quinquagenarian cultivator of the natural sciences, of the classical school. The dialogue commences in a pacific and prolix way, with the inclusion of some theology. The two interlocutors will later be rolled over by a young North American, MacFuture, who is of the opinion that the earth has been too small for quite some time and who desires to pursue further,[4] in cosmic dimensions, the discovery of America and the industrialization of his country.

In the second dialogue,[5] an old and experienced man speaks with an inexperienced student on the difficult problem of power, made yet more difficult and mysterious by the enormous augmentation of the modern means of power. The student poses more or less intelligent questions, and the old man replies with prudence and reflection. This is not a dialogue in the style of Plato. The student is no Alcibiades, and neither is the old man a Socrates. He guards himself well from forming metaphysical constructions, limiting himself to a descriptive unfolding of the dialectic immanent in each power. In our dialogue the term "demonic" ["*demoníaco*"], so much in fashion in modern dissertations on power, does not appear.[6]

In the end, the reader will see and judge. I wrote this prologue to the Spanish edition in the summer of 1961, on a tranquil estuary on the west coast of Galicia. The periodicals, the radio and the television, everything, in sum, which modern sociology calls "mass media," is filled with information on the latest miraculous feats of the Russian and

American cosmonauts. The world resonates with the triumphal clamour of scientific and technological progress.[7] But the glory that these "mass media" can confer is ephemeral. The grandeur and dignity of the human is not to be calculated according to the likelihood of winning the Nobel prize. The human is and remains a son of this earth. Against all the utopian expectations of automation and abundance, these dialogues aim to guard a prudent and sober attitude and to turn from the deceptive world of Potemkin to the reality of the human and of his earth.

C. S.

Barraña, Boiro (La Coruña)

August 1961

Dialogue on Power and Access to the Holder of Power[1]

(1954/1994/2008)

Are ye happy?
We are mighty![2]

Lord Byron[3]

Partners of the Dialogue:

Y. (a young youth; questioning)[4]

C.S. (answering)

The Intermezzo (page 38) may be spoken by a third person.

Y. Before you speak here concerning power, I must ask you something.

C.S. Please, Mr. Y.

Y. Have you yourself power or have you none?

C.S. This question is quite rightly posed. He who speaks about power ought first to say in which power-situation he finds himself.

Y. Quite so! Have you power or have you none?

C.S. I have no power. I belong to the powerless.[5]

Y. That is suspect.

C.S. Why?

Y. Because then you are presumably predisposed *against* power.[6] Anger, embitterment, *ressentiment* are foul sources of error.

C.S. And what now if I belonged among the holders of power?

Y. Then you would presumably be predisposed *for* power.[7] The interest in one's own power and in its assertion is naturally a source of error as well.

C.S. Who then has any right to speak about power?

Y. That *you* must tell me![8]

C.S. I would say: perhaps there is yet another position: that of disinterested contemplation and description.

Y. That would then be the role of the Third Man or of the free-floating intelligentsia?[9]

C.S. Intelligentsia hither, intelligentsia thither. Let us rather not begin with such subsumings. Let us attempt, first of all, to see rightly an historical manifestation that we all experience and from which we all suffer. The result will show itself.

1

Y. We are thus speaking of the power that humans exercise over other humans. Where does this terrible power stem from, which, let us say, Stalin or Roosevelt or whomever else one might like to name, have exercised over millions of other humans?

C.S. In earlier times, one would have answered to this: Power stems either from nature, or it comes from God.

Y. I fear that today power no longer appears natural to us.

C.S. I fear that as well. With respect to *nature*, we feel ourselves to be quite superior. We no longer fear it. As soon as nature becomes discomfiting for us as sickness or natural catastrophe, we hope soon to vanquish it. The human – by nature a weak form of life – has raised itself above its environment with the help of technology. It has made itself into the Lord of Nature and of all earthly forms of life. The constraints that nature tangibly laid upon the human in earlier times, through cold and heat, hunger and deprivation, wild animals and dangers of all kinds, these natural constraints manifestly recede.[10]

Y. That is true. We no longer need to fear wild animals.

C.S. The labors of Hercules seem rather modest to us today; and when today a lion or a wolf wanders into a modern metropolis, it is at most a traffic impediment and hardly even a fright to children. With respect to nature, the human today feels himself so superior that he allows himself to set up parks for nature conservation.

Y. How is it then with God?

C.S. Concerning what pertains to *God*, modern man – I mean the typical metropolitan – has in any case the sentiment that God recedes or has already receded from us. When today the name of God is mentioned, then the normal educated person of our times automatically cites the dictum of Nietzsche: God is dead.[11] Others, even better informed, cite a dictum of the French Socialist Proudhon, which pre-dated Nietzsche's dictum by forty years and asserted: He who speaks of God desires to deceive.[12]

Y. If power stems neither from nature nor from God, where does it come from then?

C.S. Then there remains only one option: the power that a human exercises over other humans, stems from the humans themselves.

Y. That's good then. We are all humans. Even Stalin was a human; even Roosevelt or whomever else one might like to name here.

C.S. That sounds really reassuring. If the power that a human exercises over others stems from nature, then it is either the power of the progenitor over its brood or the superiority of the teeth, horns, paws, claws, poison glands, and other natural weapons. Of the power of the progenitor over its brood we may well refrain from speaking. There remains, however, the power of the wolf over the lamb. A human who had power would be a wolf with respect to the humans who had no power. He who has no power feels himself to be a lamb until he himself comes into the position of having power and he may take over the role of the wolf. This confirms the Latin adage: *Homo homini lupus.*[13] In English: the human is a wolf to the human.[14]

Y. Hideous! And if power stems from God?

C.S. Then the person who exercises it is the bearer of a divine quality; he attests to something divine with his power, and one must honor, if not the man himself, then the power of God that is manifest in him. This confirms the Latin adage: *Homo homini Deus.*[15] In English: the human is a God to the human.[16]

Y. That goes too far!

C.S. However, if power stems neither from nature nor from God, then everything that concerns power and its exercise plays out only among humans. Then we humans are wholly alone amongst ourselves. The holder of power is set against the powerless, the mighty against the impotent – it's simply humans against humans.

Y. Then it's: The human is a human to the human.[17]

C.S. This confirms the Latin adage: *Homo homini homo.*

2

Y. Clearly. The human is a human to the human.[18] Only because humans are to be found who obey another human do they thereby create power. When they no longer obey him, this power ceases of its own accord.

C.S. Quite right. But why do they obey? Obedience is not arbitrary, but rather somehow motivated. Why, then, do the humans give their consent to power? In some cases out of trust, in others out of fear, sometimes out of hope, sometimes out of despair. Always, however, they need protection and they seek this protection from power. Seen from the perspective of the humans, the linkage between protection and obedience is the only explanation of power. He who does not have the power to protect someone also does not have the right to require obedience. And conversely: He who seeks protection and receives it has no right to withhold obedience.

Y. But what if the holder of power commands something reprehensible to right?[19] Then, must one not in that case withhold obedience?

C.S. Of course! But I'm not speaking of particular commands reprehensible to right,[20] but rather of a general situation in which the holder of power and those subjected to power are bound together into a political unity. Here it is the case that he who has power can uninterruptedly create effective and in no way immoral motives for obedience: through the guarantee of protection and secured existence, through education and through the interests of solidarity against others. Briefly: consensus effects power, that's right, but power also effects consensus and in no way in every case an irrational or immoral consensus.

Y. What precisely are you trying to say?[21]

C.S. I want to say that even in those cases where power is exercised with the full consent of all those subjected to it, it still retains a certain significance of its own, a surplus value, so to speak.[22] It is more than the sum of all the consents that it receives, and also more than their product. Reflect for yourself just once on the extent to which the human is constrained by social context in today's society marked by the division of labor! We saw earlier that the natural limitations recede,[23] but in their place the social limitations intrude upon the human ever more strongly and narrowly. In this way, too, the motivation for consenting to power becomes ever stronger. A modern holder of power has infinitely more means to effect the consensus to his power than had Charlemagne or Barbarossa.

3

Y. Do you wish to say that a contemporary holder of power can do what he wishes?

C.S. On the contrary. I only wish to say that power has an independent grandeur of its own, even with respect to the consensus that created it, and I would now like to show you that it is such even with respect to the holder of power himself. Power has an objective, autonomous grandeur with respect to any human individual who at any given time holds power in his hand.

Y. Now, what is here meant by "objective, autonomous grandeur"?

C.S. This means something very concrete. Realize that even the most fearsome holder of power remains bound to the limits of human *physis*, to the inadequacy of human understanding and the weaknesses of the human soul. Even the most powerful human must eat and drink like all the rest of us. He grows sick and old.

Y. But modern science provides astounding means to overcome the limitations of human nature.

C.S. Quite so. The holder of power can allow the most famous doctors and Nobel laureates to come to him. He can allow more injections to be administered to himself than to anyone else. Despite this: after several hours of work or of vice he becomes tired and falls asleep. The horrid Caracalla, the powerful Genghis Khan then lies there like a small child and quite possibly even snores.

Y. That is an image that every holder of power ought to have held before his eyes.

C.S. Yes, indeed, and this has ever been depicted with pleasure by philosophers and moralists, pedagogues and rhetoricians. However, we do not wish to linger long over it. I would like only to mention that the Englishman Thomas Hobbes, still the most modern philosopher of purely human power, for his state-construction, proceeds from this general weakness of every human individual. Hobbes builds his argument as follows: out of the weakness results endangerment, out of the endangerment, fear, out of fear, the need for security, and out of that again, the necessity of an apparatus of protection with a more or less complicated organization. But despite all of these protective measures, Hobbes says, in the right moment anyone can kill anyone else. A weak man can come into the situation where he disposes of the strongest and most powerful man. On these points the humans are really equal, insofar as they are all threatened and endangered.[24]

Y. A weak consolation.

C.S. Actually, I had the desire neither to give consolations nor to engender angst, but rather only to give an objective image of human power. Physical endangerment is only its crassest form and not even the most quotidian. Another consequence of the narrow bounds of each human individual is even better suited to show that with which we are here concerned, namely, the objective autonomy of every power with respect to the holder of power and the inescapable internal dialectic of power and impotence, into which every human holder of power falls.

Y. I can't begin to understand anything here having to do with dialectics.

C.S. We shall see. The human individual, in whose hand the great political decisions lie for an instant, can only form his will under given presuppositions and with given means. Even the most absolute prince is reliant on reports and information and dependent on his counselors. A plethora of facts and communications, recommendations and suggestions presses in upon him day by day and hour by hour. Out of this flowing, infinite sea of truth and lies, realities and possibilities even the cleverest and most powerful human can at most ladle out a few droplets.

Y. Here one really sees the splendor and misery of the absolute princes.

C.S. One sees above all the inner dialectic of human power. He who holds a lecture before the holder of power or informs him, already has a part in power, regardless of whether he is a responsible counter-signing Minister or whether he knows how to attain the ear of the holder of power in an indirect way. It suffices for him to transmit impressions and motives to the human individual in whose hand the decision lies for an instant. Thus every direct power is promptly subordinated to indirect influences. There have been holders of power who have perceived this dependence and have fallen into wrath and rage as a result of it. They then attempted to inform themselves in other ways than through their responsible counselors.

Y. In view of the corruption at court, quite rightly so.

C.S. Certainly. But regrettably they thereby only fell into new and often grotesque dependencies. In order to experience the pure truth, the Caliph Hārūn al-Rashīd[25] finally went into the taverns of Baghdad disguised as a man of the people. I don't know what he found and drank from this questionable source. Frederick the Great became so mistrustful in his old age that he continued to speak openly only with his chamber servant Fredersdorff. As a result, the chamber servant became an influential man, even though in general he remained loyal and dependable.

Y. Other holders of power end up with their chauffeur or with their lovers.

C.S. In other words: in front of every chamber of direct power an antechamber of indirect influences and powers constructs itself, a path of access to the ear, a corridor to the soul of the holder of power. There is no human power without this antechamber and without this corridor.

Y. However, one can hinder some abuses by rational institutions and constitutional specifications.

C.S. One can do that, and one should do it, too. But still no institution, however wise, no organization, however well thought out, can wholly extirpate the antechamber itself; no burst of outrage against the camarilla or the antechamber can completely dispatch with it. One cannot circumvent the antechamber itself.

Y. It appears to me to be more like a back stairwell.

C.S. Antechamber, back stairwell, foyer, lower hold: the thing itself is clear and remains the same for the dialectic of human power. In any case, in the course of world history a motley and mixed society has found itself assembled together in this antechamber of power. Here the indirect assemble themselves. Here we meet ministers and ambassadors in grand uniform, but also father-confessors and bodily physicians, adjutants and secretaries, chamber servants and mistresses. Here stands the old Fredersdorff, Frederick the Great's chamber servant, next to the Empress Augusta, Rasputin next to the Cardinal Richelieu, an *éminence grise* next to a Messalina. Sometimes clever and wise men are in this antechamber, sometimes fabulous managers and dependable *major domos*, sometimes dumb strivers and swindlers. Sometimes the antechamber is really the official chamber of state, in which the worthy Lords assemble to be allowed audience, until it is granted them. Often, however, it is only a private cabinet.

Y. Or even a hospital room, in which several friends sit about the bed of a paralyzed man and rule the world.

C.S. The more power concentrates itself in a particular position, in a particular human or a particular group of humans as in a peak, the sharper becomes the problem of the corridor and the question of access to the peak. Then so much more hefty, lock-jawed and muted becomes the battle among those who hold the antechamber in their possession and control the corridor. This battle in the fog of indirect influence is as unavoidable as it is essential for all human power. In it the internal dialectic of human power fulfills itself.

Y. But are these not the bare excrescences of a personal regime?

C.S. No. The process of constructing the corridor, which we're talking about here, plays itself out daily in minimal, infinitesimal maneuvers, on the grand scale and on the small scale, everywhere where humans exercise power over other humans. In the same measure, in which a power-chamber draws itself together, an antechamber to this power promptly organizes itself as well. Every heightening of direct power also thickens and condenses the vaporous circle of indirect influences.

Y. That can even be good, if the holder of power is not in order. I still don't see what is better here, the direct power or the indirect.

C.S. I see here the indirect only as a stage in the inescapable dialectical development of human power. The holder of power himself becomes ever more isolated the more that direct power concentrates itself in his individual person. The corridor uproots him from the ground and elevates him as if into a stratosphere, in which he is only able to reach those who rule him indirectly, while he can no longer reach all remaining humans over whom he exercises power, and they, in turn, can no longer reach him. In extreme cases this often becomes palpable in grotesque ways. However, this is only the most external consequence of an isolation of the holder of power through the unmitigated apparatus of power. The same internal logic plays out in countless maneuvers of everyday life in the constant struggle between direct power and indirect influence. No human power escapes this dialectic of self-assertion and self-alienation.

INTERMEZZO: BISMARCK AND THE MARQUIS POSA

The battle for the corridor, for access to the peak of power, is a particularly intense battle for power, through which the internal dialectic of human power and impotence is fulfilled. We must see this relationship before our eyes without rhetoric and sentimentality, but also without cynicism or nihilism. Thus, I would like to illustrate the problem through two examples.[26]

The first example is a document of constitutional history: Bismarck's petition for release [*Entlassungsgesuch*] from March 1890. It is included in the third volume of Bismarck's *Thoughts and Reminiscences* [*Gedanken und Erinnerungen*] and treated there thoroughly. It is in all respects, in its design, in its trajectory of thought and its intonation, in that which it articulates as in that on which it is silent, the well thought-out work of a great master of the art of state.[27] It was Bismarck's last official act and it was devised and stylized with full reflection as a document for posterity. The old, experienced Reich's Chancellor, the creator of the Empire, confronts the inexperienced heir, the young King and Kaiser Wilhelm II. Between both of them there existed many material oppositions and differences of opinion in questions of internal and external politics. But the kernel of the petition for release [*Entlassungsgesuch*], the real point of contention, is something purely formal: the conflict concerning the question of how the Chancellor may inform himself and how the King and Kaiser should inform himself. Here Bismarck claims full liberty with regard to with whom he converses and who is to be received by him in his home. However, to the King and Kaiser he denies the right of giving audience to the counsel of a Minister when Bismarck, the Minister-President, is not present. Thus the problem of immediate audience with the King becomes the core point of the Bismarckian petition for release [*Entlassungsgesuch*]. With it begins the tragedy of the Second Reich. The problem of audience with the King is the core problem of every monarchy as such, because it is the problem of access to the peak. Even the Baron vom Stein[28] wore himself out in the battle against secret cabinet meetings. On the old and eternal problem of access to the peak even a Bismarck had to fail.

Let's draw the second example from Schiller's dramatic poem *Don Carlos*. Here a great dramatist demonstrates his vision for the essence of power. The plot of the drama turns on the question: who has immediate access to the King, to the absolute monarch Philip II? He who has immediate access to the King partakes of his power. Up until this point the father-confessor and the general, the Duke of Alba, held and possessed the antechamber of power and blocked access to the King. Now there appears a third man, the Marquis Posa, and both of the others immediately recognize the danger. At the end of the third act the drama achieves the high-point of its tension, in the last line of the act, as the King commands: The Knight – that is the Marquis Posa – shall henceforth be allowed an audience unannounced! This works to great dramatic effect, not only on the spectators, but rather also on all of the persons active in the drama itself. "That is really too much," Don Carlos says, when he learns of it, "too much, truly too much"[29]; and the father-confessor Domingo says tremulously to the Duke of Alba: "Our times are past."[30] After this high-point, the sudden turn to tragedy sets in, the *peripeteia* of the grand drama. As a result of his success in finding immediate access to the holder of power, the unfortunate Marquis Posa is struck with a deadly blow. What he for his part – had he been able to assert his position with the King – might have stirred up with the father-confessor and the general, we do not know.

4

C.S. However impressive these examples may be, don't forget, dear Mr. Y., in what respect all of this concerns us; namely as a moment in the internal dialectic of human power. There are still some other questions, which we could discuss here, for example, the abysmal problem of *succession* in power, whether this is dynastic or democratic or charismatic.[31] But it ought now to be clear enough what is meant by this dialectic.

Y. Still, I only see the splendor and misery of humans; you're always speaking of an inner dialectic. For this reason I would like now to pose a very simple question: If that power, which is exercised by humans, stems not from God and not from nature, but is rather an internal human concern, is it then good or bad, or what is it?

C.S. This question is more dangerous than you perhaps surmise. For most humans would answer with the greatest self-evidence: Power is good, when *I* have it,[32] and it is evil, when my enemy has it.

Y. Let us rather say: Power is in itself neither good nor bad; it is neutral in itself; it is that which the human makes of it:

in the hands of a good human it is good, in the hands of an evil human, it is evil.

C.S. And who decides in the concrete case whether a human is good or evil? The holder of power himself or another? That one has power means above all that he himself decides. That belongs to his power. Should another decide, then precisely this other has power or in any case lays claim to it.[33]

Y. Then power in itself appears to be quite neutral.

C.S. He who believes in an omnipotent and beneficent God cannot explain power as evil, nor can he explain it as neutral. The Apostle of Christianity, Saint Paul, says famously in the Letter to the Romans: All power is from God.[34] The Pope Saint Gregory the Great,[35] the exemplar of a papal shepherd of the people, expresses himself concerning this matter with the greatest clarity and decisiveness. Listen for once to what he says:

God is the highest power and the highest being. All power is from him and is and remains in its essence divine and good. Should the devil have power, then even this power, in so far as it is power, is divine and good. Only the will of the devil is evil. But despite this ever evil, devilish will, power in itself remains divine and good.[36]

Thus speaks the great Saint Gregory. He says: Only the *will* to power is evil, but power itself is always good.[37]

Y. That is really unbelievable. Here, however, I find more illuminating Jacob Burckhardt, who famously said: Power, in itself, is evil.

C.S. Let us for once look somewhat more closely at this famed maxim of Burckhardt. The decisive place in his *World-Historical Observations* runs as follows:

And now it's manifest – one thinks here of Louis XIV, of Napoleon and of the revolutionary people's governments – that power in itself is evil (Schlosser), that without regard to any religion the right of selfishness, which one denies to the individual, will be attributed to the State.

The name Schlosser was inserted in parentheses by Burckhardt's nephew Jacob Oeri, the editor of the *World-Historical Observations*, be it as documentary proof or be it as authority.

Y. Schlosser, that's a brother-in-law of Goethe.

C.S. The brother-in-law of Goethe was Johann Georg Schlosser. Here, the reference is to Friedrich Christoph Schlosser, the author of an humanitarian world-history, whom Jacob Burckhardt gladly cited in his lectures. But both, or rather all three in my view, Jacob Burckhardt and both Schlossers taken together, fail to even approximate Gregory the Great.

Y. But, after all, we no longer live in the early Middle Ages! I am certain that for most people today Burckhardt is more illuminating than Gregory the Great.

C.S. Manifestly, something essential related to power must have changed since the time of Gregory the Great. Then, too, in the time of Gregory the Great there were wars and atrocities of all kinds. On the other hand, the holders of power who, according to Burckhardt, particularly ought to illustrate the evil of power – Louis XIV, Napoleon and the French revolutionary regimes – are already quite modern holders of power.

Y. They weren't even motorized. And they had yet even to *conceive* of anything related to atomic bombs and hydrogen bombs.

C.S. We may not consider Schlosser and Burckhardt as saints, but still we may consider them as pious men, who would not have expressed themselves frivolously.

Y. How, then, is it then possible that a pious man of the seventh century held power to be good, while pious men of the nineteenth and twentieth centuries held power for evil? Here something essential must have changed.

C.S. I believe that in the last century the essence of human power has laid itself bare to us in a quite particular way. It is indeed curious that the thesis of power being evil has spread precisely since the nineteenth century. We had thought that the problem of power would be solved or at least defused if power stemmed neither from God nor from nature, but were rather something that humans make wholly among themselves. What then should the human still fear if God is dead and the wolf isn't even frightful to children anymore? But precisely since the epoch, in which the humanization of power appeared to have run itself to completion – since the French Revolution – the conviction now spreads irresistibly that power is in itself evil. The maxim *God is dead* and the other maxim *Power in itself is evil* both stem from the same period and the same situation.[38] Fundamentally they both articulate the same thing.

5

Y. Actually, that is still in some need of an explanation.

C.S. In order to understand correctly the essence of human power, as it reveals itself in our contemporary situation, we shall do our best to acquaint ourselves with a relation discovered by the aforementioned Englishman Thomas

Hobbes, still the most modern philosopher of purely human power. He expressed and articulated this relation in all its exactness, and after him we shall name it the "Hobbesian Dangerousness-Relation." Hobbes says: The human is to other humans, from whom he believes himself to be endangered, as much more dangerous than any animal as the weapons of the human are more dangerous than those of the animal. That is a clear and specific relation.

Y. Oswald Spengler has already said that the human is a predator.

C.S. Pardon! The Dangerousness-Relation, which Thomas Hobbes set up, has not the least to do with the thesis of Oswald Spengler. Hobbes, by contrast, presupposes that the human is *no* animal, but rather something wholly other, on the one hand less, on the other hand much more. The human is able to compensate, to overcompensate in a monstrous way for his biological weakness and inadequacy through technological inventions. Now pay attention. Around 1650, as Hobbes articulated this metrical relation, the weapons of the human – bow and arrow, ax and sword, rifles and canons – were already quite superior and dangerous enough in comparison with the paws of a lion or the teeth of a wolf. But today the dangerousness of the technological means has escalated boundlessly. Consequently the dangerousness of humans to other humans has correspondingly escalated as well. As a result the distinction between power and powerlessness is growing in such a boundless way, that it is drawing the concept of the human itself into fully new modes of questioning.

Y. That I don't understand.

C.S. Listen. Who is actually the human here? The one who produces and deploys these modern means of annihilation, or the one, against whom they are deployed? It doesn't help us at all if one says: Power is like technology, which is neither good nor bad in itself, but rather neutral; it is consequently what the human makes of it. That would evade the real difficulty of facing the question of who decides what is good and what is evil. The power of the modern means of annihilation exceeds the force of the human individuals who invent those means and who bring them to be deployed just as much as the capacities of modern machines and techniques exceed the force of human muscles and brains. In this stratosphere, in this domain of ultrasound, the good or evil human will doesn't even tag along. The human arm that holds the atom bomb, the human brain that innervates the muscles of the human arm is, in the decisive moment, less an appendage of the individual isolated human than a prosthesis, a part of the technical and social apparatus that produces the atom bomb and deploys it. The power of the individual holder of power is here only the perspiration of a situation that results from a system of incalculably enhanced division of labor.

Y. Is it then not great the way that we today penetrate into the stratosphere, into the domain of ultrasound, or out of the world's atmosphere, and that we have machines that calculate faster and better than any human brain?

C.S. In this "we" the actual question conceals itself. It is indeed no longer the human qua human, but rather a chain-reaction unleashed from the human that achieves all of this. By exceeding the limits of human *physis*, it also transcends all inter-personal measures of every thinkable power of humans over humans. It also overturns the relation between protection and obedience. Power has slipped out of human hands even more than has technology, and the humans who exercise power over others with the help of such technological means are no longer alone with those who are subject to their power.

Y. But those who have invented and produced the modern means of annihilation are still only human.

C.S. Even set against those who effected it the power that they hold is an objective, autonomous eminence, which infinitely exceeds the narrow physical, intellectual and animating capacities of its individual human inventors. In the invention of these means of annihilation, the inventors work unconsciously on the establishment of a new Leviathan. Already the modern, thoroughly well-organized, European state of the sixteenth and seventeenth centuries was a technological and artistic product, a Super-Human [*Über-Mensch*] created by humans out of humans set together with one another, which in the image of the Leviathan as the large human, the μάκρος ἄνθρωπος, and the little humans producing it, the isolated individual, the μίκρος ἄνθροπος, confronted with a Super-Power [*Über-Macht*]. In this sense the well-functioning European state of early modern period was the first modern machine and simultaneously the concrete presupposition of all further technological machines. It was the machine of machines, the *machina machinarum*, a Super-Human [*Über-Mensch*] compiled of humans gathered together, which comes into existence via human consensus and yet, in the moment that it is present, exceeds all human consensus. It is precisely because this issue concerns a power organized by humans that Burckhardt feels that this power is evil in itself. For this reason, in his famous maxim Burckhardt does not refer to Nero or Genghis Khan but rather to the typically modern European holders of power: Louis XIV, Napoleon and the popular revolutionary regimes.

Y. Perhaps further scientific discoveries could change all of this and put it back in order.

C.S. That would be good. But how would you like to change the fact that today power and impotence are no longer set over and against one another eye-to-eye and no longer gaze at each other from human to human? The human masses who feel themselves exposed to the modern means of annihilation know above all that they are impotent. The reality of power greatly exceeds the reality of the humans.

I'm not saying that the power of humans over humans is good. I'm also not saying that it's evil. Least of all am I saying that it's neutral. And I would shame myself as a thinking person to say that it's good when *I* have it and evil when my enemy has it. I say only that power is an independent reality set against everyone, even the holder of power, and that it draws him into its dialectic. Power is stronger that any will to power, stronger than any human good and happily stronger than any human evil as well.

Y. It is indeed reassuring that power as an objective magnitude ought to be stronger than all the evil of the humans, who exercise power; but, on the other hand, it is unsatisfying that that it ought also to be stronger than the goodness of humans. That is not positive enough for me. Hopefully, you are not a Machiavellian.

C.S. That I definitely am not. By the way, Machiavelli himself was also not a Machiavellian.

Y. That's too paradoxical for me.

C.S. I find it quite simple. If Machiavelli had been a Machiavellian, then he would definitely not have written books that would have placed him in a bad light. He would have written pious and devotional books, most likely an *Anti-Machiavell.*[39]

Y. That would naturally have been cleverer. But there must nonetheless be practical applications of your conception. What then should we actually do now?

C.S. What should we do? Do you recall the beginning of our dialogue? You put the question to me of whether I myself have power or not. Now we could for once turn the tables by my asking you: Have you yourself power, or have you none?

Y. Apparently you would like to evade my question concerning the practical application.

C.S. On the contrary, I only wanted to provide myself the chance of giving a meaningful answer to your question. When one inquires after practical applications with respect to power, then it makes quite a difference whether he himself has power or has none.

Y. Surely. But you keep saying that power is something objective and stronger than any human who holds it in hand. There must be some examples of practical applications.

C.S. There are infinitely many, both for those who have power, as well as for those who have none. It would indeed already be a great achievement if one could bring it about that the real political power could appear publicly and visibly upon the political stage. To the holder of power, for example, I would recommend never to appear in public without ministerial costume or similar costumery. To one of the powerless I would say: Don't believe that you are good just because you have no power. And if he suffered because he had no power, I would remind him that the will to power is as self-destructive as the will to lust or the will to other things that render one insatiable. To the members of a constitutional assembly or one consulting on the writing of a constitution-counselling assembly I would lay the problem of access to the peak of power on their heart, so that they would be unable to conceive that they could organize the administration of their land according to some schema as if it were a long-familiar job. Briefly, you see, there are very many practical applications.

Y. But the human! Where does the human remain?

C.S. Everything that a human – with or without power – thinks or does passes through the corridor of human consciousness and of other individual human capacities.

Y. Then the human is a human to the human!

C.S. That he is indeed. However this is only the case in a concrete sense. For example, this means: the human Stalin is to the human Trotsky a Stalin, and the human Trotsky is to the human Stalin a Trotsky.

Y. Shall that be your last word?

C.S. No. With this I only wanted to tell you that the fine formula: the human is a human to the human a human – *homo homini homo* – is no solution, but rather only the beginning of our problematic. I mean this critically, but in a thoroughly affirmative way, in the sense of the verse:

> *To be human, nonetheless, remains a decision.*[40]
> That shall be my last word.

BACKWARD GLANCE AT THE COURSE OF THE DIALOGUE

Dialogue on New Space[1]
(1955/1958/1994)

Partners of the Dialogue:[2]

A. – *Altmann* (Old historian)

N . – *Neumeyer* (Chemical Physicist)

F. – *MacFuture* (North American)

A. We wished to begin with the opposition between land and sea and then to talk about the distinction between terrestrial and maritime existence.[3] In this matter, may I allow myself an indiscreet question, dear Mr. Neumeyer?

N. If it is not all too indiscreet, honorable Mr. Altmann, by all means!

A. Hopefully it is not all too indiscreet. I only wished to ask you whether you read the Bible occasionally?

N. Do you mean the Old Testament or the New?

A. I hadn't even thought of such fine distinctions. I meant, wholly generally, the Bible, the book of books, both the Old and the New Testament.

N. In relation to the Bible, I would like to say something to you, Mr. Altmann: I very much esteem the Bible and respect it thoroughly. But I am a scientifically thinking human and the Bible is – with all due respect – no scientific book. Neither the Old nor the New Testament. That does not exclude the fact that I occasionally open it up and also find there something edifying. But I must ask: what does that have to do with our theme of land and sea?

A. The Bible, Mr. Neumeyer, is concerned from beginning to end with the opposition between land and sea. It is filled with precisely this opposition.

N. Very improbable!

A. You only need to open up the beginning of the Bible and to read there how God created the world. That is the first chapter of the history of creation from Genesis, the first book of Moses, chapter one. There it is related that God created the world through a succession of several separations: first, he separates light from darkness; then he separates the fixity of the heavens, the firmament, from the waters over and under the firmament; then he separates the dry land from the sea and allots the dry land as a dwelling to the humans. Thus, there were three separations or partitions.

N. Beautiful. But we didn't wish to converse about theological matters.

A. We wished to converse about the opposition between land and sea and the distinction between terrestrial and maritime existence, and here we find in one of the oldest and holiest books of humanity a very decisive *prise de position* for a purely terrestrial existence. According to the Bible, God allotted the fixed land to the humans as a dwelling place, while he pressed back the sea to the boundaries of this dwelling place. There it lurks as a standing danger and threat to the humans. God's goodness holds back the sea so that it doesn't engulf us, as in a flood. The sea is foreign and inimical to the humans. It is no living space [*Lebensraum*] for the humans. Living space [*Lebensraum*] for the humans is, according to the Bible, only dry land.

N. In this matter, the word "living space" ["*Lebensraum*"], honorable Mr. Altmann, sounds somewhat suspect. It smacks of modern geopolitics. I would bet that the word "living space" ["*Lebensraum*"] does not appear in the Bible.

A. That would be a question of translation. I personally take the word "living space" ["*Lebensraum*"] from an outstanding theological commentary on the history of creation, namely the third volume of the *Dogmatics* of the highly esteemed, justly world-renowned Basel theologian, Professor Dr. Karl Barth.[4] But we don't wish to fight about words here. In the fact of the matter it's clear that according to the biblical history of creation only the fixed land is the dwelling place of the human, or put more clearly: only the fixed land is the abode of the human. On the contrary, the sea, the ocean, is an uncanny monstrosity on the brink of the inhabited world, a chaotic beast, a great serpent, a dragon, a leviathan.

N. Most honorable Mr. Altmann, for once please pay attention to your own words and terms, as you are here deploying them: on the one hand, you call the earth the abode of the human, on the other hand, you speak of the sea as a chaotic monstrosity, a serpent, a dragon, a leviathan. Abode, serpent, dragon, leviathan – these are all manifestly mythic images; they bear the stamp of the unscientific upon their brow. I shall tell you what the biblical account of creation is about: it is about the mythic world image of a terrestrial culture, that is to say, a culture essentially determined by the land. The Old Testament received its report of creation from the Babylonians, perhaps from other peoples and cultures older still. In any case, its world-image was purely terrestrial and not maritime. The notion of fixed land as an abode of the human and the notion of the sea as an inimical monstrosity are to be explained in this fashion. Basically, all this is quite simple.

A. Indeed, dear Mr. Neumeyer, it is surely quite simple. But, for this reason, it needn't be false or insignificant.

N. No, but it is unscientific and fully superseded. It is antiquated, an anachronism, in the best case an interesting museum piece. Peoples of a purely terrestrial existence, like herdsmen or tillers of the land, think in a typical way up from the soil and have a religious dread in the face of the sea. Most of the ancient cultures known to us are terrestrial and not maritime. The Old Testament angst before the sea doesn't surprise me in the least. I would, however, be interested to know how the New Testament is arranged in this matter. I suspect that the angst in the face of the sea is not so strongly pronounced. The Apostle Paul, as far as I know, undertook great sea voyages in the Mediterranean.

A. In the New Testament, Christ strolls upon the sea. He quelled the Leviathan. Yet, precisely here it is recapitulated that for the New Testament as well the sea is something uncanny and evil. At the end of the last book, in the Revelation of Saint John, there is a sketch of how the new earth appears, the earth purified of sin and evil. It is written in chapter twenty-one of this apocalypse of Saint John: Then I saw a new heaven and a new earth, for the first heaven and the first earth had passed away, and there was no longer any sea.[5] Have you heard? The sea was no more! Upon the purified and transfigured earth there is no ocean. Along with sin and evil, the sea disappears as well. That is the end of the New Testament. From the account of creation from the first book of Moses to the end of the Revelation of Saint John, the Bible maintains the opposition between land and sea.

N. For me, too, this passage in the Revelation of Saint John is perfectly clear. It is concerned with the old mythic angst that land-dwellers have in the face of the sea. Herdsmen and tillers of the land think of the earth as a tent or a house in which they dwell, surrounded by pasture or a garden. For them, this is the habitable world of humans. On the shores of this habitable world there surges the ocean, the terrible world-serpent. At the end of days, the world-serpent shall be slain, and there shall emerge a blessed new earth freed from war and crime, upon which there is no more sea. This is an old dream; for herdsmen and tillers of the land, a beautiful dream as well. In the renowned poem of a great Roman poet, in Virgil's fourth ecologue, this dream also found its expression. Virgil claims that in that happy end-time of undisturbed peace there would, above all, be no more commerce by sea. I could name for you still more examples. But what would it matter? All of this is the ideological progeny of a purely terrestrial existence; the fantasies of shepherds and peasants; myth – pardon me – poetry, poesy – Rilke.

1

A. What, then, does the opposition between land and sea mean for your purely scientific interpretation?

N. Scientifically, I find the opposition fully antiquated. It is a petty vestige of the old doctrine of the four elements: earth, water, air and fire. A primitive natural philosophy contrived these four as kinds of basic elements. As is well known, element means: a material that our chemical means cannot further decompose. Today every schoolchild knows that neither earth nor water nor air nor fire is an element. Already at the beginning of our century, modern natural science discovered around ninety wholly other materials that chemical methods could not decompose further.

A. Thus the matter appears scientifically. And now you ought to look for just a minute at world history. World history is a continuous confrontation between land powers and sea powers. Think about the Thirty Years War between Sparta and Athens, which ends with the victory of the land power, Sparta; or, the Hundred Years War between Rome and Carthage, which, again, ends with the victory of the land power, Rome; or, finally, think about the over three hundred years' confrontation between England and the European continental states – in sequence, Spain, Holland, France and Germany – a confrontation that ends with the victory of the sea power, England. Thus world history appears. A great historical work by the French Admiral Castex[6] characteristically bears the title, *The Sea against the Land, La mer contre la terre.*[7]

N. That is the book of an admiral. That is how world history appears to admirals. For admirals, world history is a history of sea wars and sea battles. The French Admiral Castex, the American Admiral Mahan,[8] the German Admiral Tirpitz;[9] all marine professionals, departmental politicians. It's no wonder[10] that they think of world-history from the perspective of their job.

A. Every human does that to a greater or a lesser extent.

N. Bad enough, since that's unscientific.

A. I shall not ask you, dear Mr. Neumeyer, how you think about world history. Chemistry and physics are, in the end, also a job. In any case, the opposition between land and sea also contains natural scientific ingredients. Land and sea and air are different aggregate states. They are physically, meteorologically, geologically and geographically different and consequently entail different environments for the life forms that live in their domains. That again causes biological contrasts, which you cannot well deny. The human is a mammal; it is not a fish, which breathes through gills. That, too, ought to be of interest to a natural scientist.

N. Of course, here there are numerous differences, in particular biologically interesting differences between terrestrial and maritime existence, although we shall leave aside amphibians like the frog or abnormalities like the whale. From out of such biological differences there emerges no opposition between humans, and, above all, there emerge no tensions of enmity between peoples and powers, no world history with land wars and sea wars. Between the animals of the land and those of the sea there is no natural enmity; there is not even a natural tension. Normally, they don't even concern themselves with one another. The fish remains in the water and the land animal remains upon the earth. Each knows where it belongs. Even among the land animals, the great hunters among them – the lion, the tiger, the bear – have their natural hunting grounds; they do not run up against one another in the clearing. The battle for nutrition is mostly played out between life forms in the same domain–not, however, between land and sea. As is well known, the great fish devour the small ones and the life forms of the land or of the air do not behave much better. There is no space at all for an enmity that is defined generally through the opposition between land and sea. I know that politicians and historians of the nineteenth century depicted the oppositions between Russia and England as a battle between a bear and a whale. That is pure nonsense. No bear is so without instinct as to allow itself to be drawn into battle with a whale, and still less so does a whale battle with a bear.

A. Applied to humans, this clean separation between land and sea ought to entail that sea wars only occur between sea peoples and land wars only occur between terrestrial peoples. Remarkably, the opposite is the case when the world historical tensions reach a certain degree of intensity. Not animals, but indeed humans, and *only* humans, conduct land *and* sea wars with one another. Whenever enmity between great powers reaches a climax, the martial confrontation plays itself out simultaneously in both domains, and the war becomes a land *and* sea war on both sides. Every power is compelled to follow the opponent into the other element. When the air is brought in as a third dimension, the war becomes an aerial war on both sides. Therefore, it seems to me to be sensible to continue to speak here of the elements land and sea. When a world-historical opposition approaches its climax, then on both sides all material forces, all forces of soul, and all intellectual forces are brought to bear in the conflict to the greatest extreme. Then the battle extends across the whole environment of the participating powers. At this point, the elementary opposition between land and sea is itself brought into the confrontation. The war then appears as the war of the land against the sea and the war of the sea against the land; in other words: as a war of the elements against one another. You need only open your eyes and look at our own contemporary world situation. We live today under the pressure of a global tension, of an opposition of East and West. Manifestly, this contemporary opposition between East and West is simultaneously an opposition between land and sea.

N. East and West are purely geographic concepts and no rational ground for enmity; East and West – that does not even yield a polar tension. As is well known, the earth has a North- and a South pole, but no East- and West pole. In relation to the United States of America, Russia and China are the West.

A. Very well. Now, does that make the tension today between East and West any less real? And above all: is it not the case that the gigantic landmasses of Russia and China lie on the side of the East and that the monstrous surfaces of the world seas, of the Atlantic and Pacific Oceans, lie on the side of the West? I did not say that the opposition between land and sea is the *reason* for today's global tension between East and West. But he who desires to reflect upon the deeper causes of that tension cannot ignore that since Yalta or at least since the Atlantic Pact of 1949, there has existed an elemental and global tension that reflects itself in the opposition of the elements land and sea and that to a great extent corresponds to this opposition.

N. What, then, in your opinion, is the true or deeper reason for this contemporary global tension between East and West that presses upon us all?

A. I first want to give you the reply of a significant English scientist, without identifying myself with it. It concerns the great geographer Sir Halford Mackinder,[11] who articulated his view over thirty years ago in a brilliant text: *Democratic Ideals and Reality* (1919). For Mackinder, the monstrous landmass of Asia is a giant island and the heartland of the earth. Human civilization develops on the coasts of the sea. According to Mackinder, the great masses of population from the barbarian heartland constantly press upon the coasts and seek to overrun civilization. According to this English geographer, the opposition between land and sea in its innermost core is an opposition between civilization and barbarism, between unfreedom and freedom, with civilization and freedom standing on the side of the sea and the coasts.

N. That's very exciting. But here I would no longer discourse about elements. Today, the sea is just another a field of human activity as are the land and the air as well. In the times of sailing ships things were otherwise. Then, ships were on the high seas for months and years and cut off from any contact with the land. There one could still speak of an element. Today, by contrast, every ship in every part of the ocean is reachable daily and hourly. Already in comparison with the age of the sailing ship, the world of the sea changed for humanity; it lost its elemental character. To me it seems that everything that you draw into world-historical phenomena or constructions, including the highly interesting theory of the English geographer Mackinder, is only the form of appearance of an historically bounded picture of the world.

A. Careful, dear Mr. Neumeyer! Ultimately, your own picture of the world is probably somehow bound to an historical situation. Even exact natural science and even unencumbered technology do not stand outside of history. You yourself, dear Mr. Neumeyer, several minutes ago did away with the ancient conceptions of land and sea as an anachronism, as a dream and myth of herdsmen and tillers of the land. Do you perchance believe that physicists, chemists, and technicians dreamed no dreams, produced no myths and were immune to anachronisms?

N. Ah, so. I see where you wish to go with this, honorable Mr. Altmann. You now wish to come at me historically. You are now working with the so-called historical sense and with historical dialectics. That is the notorious sixth sense, which that ingenious bird of ill omen, *Hegel*,[12] infiltrated into the poor Germans.

A. Did you not yourself work earlier with the historical sense, when you declared the ancient conceptions of land and sea anachronistic? Anachronistic, that is to say: no longer appropriate to the time and the situation. You yourself definitely do not wish to renounce being in step with our times, i.e. being appropriate to the time and to the situation.

2

F. Pardon me, gentlemen, for inserting myself into your dialogue at this moment. I am MacFuture. I have been listening to you and have attempted to follow your dispute concerning land and sea. Up until now I have remained silent.

A. and N. We have been wondering about that ourselves for quite some time now.[13]

F. But now you must permit me to interject. Indeed, I find you both, both you, honorable Mr. Altmann, with your historical sense, but also you, dear Mr. Neumeyer, with your rather classical natural scientificity – I find you both, excuse me, outdated. Even the distinction between nature and history has long been superseded. We have been living for over ten years in the age of atomic energy. Both of you have not yet really come to terms with that. All our notions of space and time, of nature and history are atomically altered. And as for the so-called elements – it doesn't matter how you use the word – I can tell you that today we have already come so far that we can manufacture artificial elements. Artificial elements, imagine that! Here all your beautiful distinctions melt – the distinction between land and sea, terrestrial and maritime, nature and history – all that melts like fat in the glowing oven.

A. A hearty welcome, dear MacFuture! You are the right man. You intervene in the right moment. It's wonderful that you've alerted us to humanity's completely altered situation and have led our dialogue over to another level. Our questions are not thereby resolved but rather dissolved. Now we only have to grasp that we must pose wholly new questions and we must pay heed that we correctly recognize the new questions. In other words: we must ask what the new question is; we stand – if I may formulate it so pointedly for once – before the question concerning a question.

F. For me that is much too complicated. I am for simplification and disentanglement. Questions here, questions there. This concerns simple facts. He who has not grasped where the journey is going misses the connection and simply does not travel any further. In any case, there are humans who first grasp the age of atomic energy when a hydrogen bomb falls upon their heads.

N. By God's will, MacFuture! Hopefully, you don't intend to enlighten us by coming with atomic bombs yourself? I am, as you will have noted, a scientifically thinking human and I greet all progress. But I cannot get excited about this type of argumentation. There must always remain something that is human. There are insurmountable moral boundaries for every human activity, even – as I would like to add expressly – for science.

F. It's self-evident that we hold ourselves strictly to the norms of morality. But do you wish for this reason to erect boundaries to free scientific research? That would be the end of our civilization! We could just as well have remained in the deepest depths of the Middle Ages. No, gentlemen, the freedom of research is holy and boundless.

N. Righteous heaven![14] I am myself a scientist and am truly the last person who would lay a finger on the unconditional freedom of research. That would be to saw off the branch upon which I perch. Research may not be restricted in any way. I was only thinking of certain consequences, of the implementation of certain discoveries and of securing against abuse.

F. That is self-evident, Mr. Neumeyer, abuse shall be unreservedly hindered. It would indeed be unbelievable if any random person X were allowed to busy themselves with explosive materials. That's clear. Let that be only my concern. These are problems of security that we here do better to bracket off. Just now it was only my wish to bring your dialogue on land and sea up to date with current events. Don't you see that humans and earth, land and sea, air and fire have changed? Indeed, every schoolchild knows how laughably small our earth has become and how human forces ascend to infinity. With the help of our machines we bring about outputs and velocities that exceed every human capacity of sense and all muscular strength. With the help of our apparatuses we calculate numbers and numerical sequences that surpass the capacity of a human brain. Thus, we have found ourselves for quite some time in a new world, in a Beyond, if you will. You only have yet to notice it.

N. I as a scientist must concede that you are perfectly correct, MacFuture.

A. And I, as the man with the historical sense, must ask a further question.

F. By God's will, hopefully not the previously mentioned question concerning the question.

A. Regrettably, by God, precisely this question concerning the great question.

F. Here my brain relents.

A. Then allow yourself to build a cybernetic apparatus that grasps and answers this question for you.

N. Couldn't you spare us this question, honorable Mr Altmann? Wouldn't it be more correct if we proceeded now toward the solution of practical matters? Aren't new infinite spaces actually opening up in the cosmos? We are actually reaching into the stratosphere. Today we already know the moon so precisely that there we can readily distinguish between elevations of thirty meters. If, for example, pyramids or skyscrapers or the Cologne Cathedral stood there, we would be able to see these things clearly. Further unimagined discoveries are imminent. Do you wish to renounce such a call from a new world? With respect for your historical sense, honorable Mr. Altmann, the historical sense ought not to make one blind when a new world opens itself.

3

A. What is actually new here? And who is blind here? That would still require a moment to prove. May I still allow myself one question?

F. If it isn't your question concerning the question yet again.

A. It doesn't go that far yet. I want to return to our contemporary world situation, to the opposition between East and West, which is manifestly at the same time an opposition between land and sea. What, in your opinion, MacFuture, is hidden behind today's world opposition? What is the core of the global dualism, which presses upon us all?

F. That I can tell you quite precisely. The contemporary global opposition between East and West is concerned with nothing other than different levels and degrees of technical industrialization. The West, with its maritime peoples, has a certain advantage technologically and industrially. This is related to the industrial revolution and the progress of technology. In the maritime West, the industrial revolution has progressed further than in the terrestrial East. That is all. This East must allow itself to be developed by us.

A. That appears to me to be the case as well. Accordingly, we have good common ground for our further discussion and shall do best to remain with the theme of the industrial revolution and technological progress. With this, we ought to guard ourselves from the frightful and fruitless strife concerning the value and non-value of technology, which is dominant today. As you know: some people damn technology and assert it to be unholy and the work of the devil; others celebrate it and consider it as the way to paradise. We would do better to leave aside this whole chaotic strife. Instead of this, let us ask dispassionately: where does this industrial revolution come from, which is our fate? What is its origin and its home? What is its point of departure and its innermost drive?

N. We all know where the industrial revolution comes from. It comes from England in the eighteenth century. The dates are to be found in all school textbooks: the first coal furnace in 1735; the first cast-iron steel in 1740; the first steam-engine in 1768; the first modern factory in Nottingham in

1769; the first spinning jenny in 1770; the mechanical loom in 1786, and so on, up to the first steam locomotive in 1825.

A. No question, the industrial revolution stems from England. In this respect, it appears important to me that it stems from the *island* England.[15]

N. Do you already wish to conduct geopolitics again? What does this have to do with the island England? It could be a pure coincidence that the industrial revolution emerged on an island.

A. I don't mean just any island. There are a thousand islands on which no industrial revolution emerged. Sicily, for example, is also an island, even one with old sulfur deposits. The island England must have fulfilled a particular historical condition when the industrial revolution emerged precisely there and precisely in the eighteenth century. I shall also soon tell you wherein the historical peculiarity of this island England consisted in the eighteenth century and what made for its uniqueness and incomparability. The island England, on which the industrial revolution emerged, was really no random island. It underwent a very definite historical development and took an astounding step. It underwent the transformation from a terrestrial to a maritime existence in the immediately preceding two centuries.

N. Hadn't the English already engaged in shipping during the Middle Ages?

A. Naturally they did, but much less than some other peoples, less than the Portuguese, less than the Basques, less than the Venetians or the Hanseatic League. Up until the sixteenth century, the island England was no more than a severed-off piece of the European continent, with its countenance turned toward the fixed land. Still in the fifteenth century, the English knights in France took a good haul of booty, as did the knights of other lands as well. Just think about the age of the Maid of Orléans! Up until the sixteenth century, the English were a people of shepherds who sold their wool to Flanders, where it was worked into cloth. And this people of shepherds metamorphosed in the sixteenth and seventeenth centuries into a people of sea-dogs. Now the island turns its countenance away from the continent and glances out upon the great seas of the world. It lifts anchor and becomes the bearer of power over an oceanic world empire.

N. England's emergence as the greatest sea power of the world took more than two hundred years. I doubt whether most English people acted according to a plan.

A. That may well be. As is well known, the great English historian Seeley[16] even said: "In a fit of absence of mind we conquered the world."[17] But why don't you try that just once! Here we are speaking of the decisive onset of the historical epoch that has an industrial revolution as its content. It was only relatively late, only after 1570, that the English success-fully inserted themselves into the age of the great discoveries. They were also late in taking part in the great land appro-priations in America and Asia. Despite this they outflanked all of their European rivals: the Portuguese, the Spanish, the Dutch and the French, and above all: the English alone completed the great sea appropriation [*Seenahme*]; they alone achieved mastery over the world's seas.

N. Now, was this an accident or was it deserved, or what was it?

A. Despite the previously cited "absence of mind," it was no accident and also not undeserved. But it was not deserved in the sense that the English of the sixteenth and seventeenth centuries were morally better or intellectually superior humans in comparison with their rivals, the Portuguese, the Spanish, the Dutch and the French of that period. They only brought to pass something that none of their European rivals brought to pass: they heeded the historical call of the time and followed it.

N. And what was this call of the time?

A. It was the call of the world oceans opening themselves. That distinguishes the English of the seventeenth century from all the seafaring peoples who remained in an inland sea, who did not dare to venture out onto the oceans, thus, it distinguishes them, for example, from the ancient Greeks, who – as Plato says of them somewhat hatefully – lie on the coasts like frogs, or from the Venetians. These peoples remained thalassic. The English became oceanic. At that time, in the age of the great European discoveries, many able and even excellent peoples either did not heed the call of the oceans opening themselves or they did not follow the call or they followed it and yet finally remained upon the shore. The Spanish conquered an entire overseas continent, but they exhausted themselves in this great land appropriation, they became no oceanic sea people; they remained upon the soil of their traditional terrestrial existence. Others, like the Portuguese or later the Dutch, followed the call of the oceans opening themselves, but their foundation was too small and the final separation from the continent was not achieved. Here, the history of France is particularly tragic. No one heeded the call of the new oceans more than the French seafarers, no one followed it more boldly. But France decided for Roman Catholicism in the seventeenth century, and at that time this meant: for the land and the earth. All European discoverers took only land. England took the sea. Only England dared to make the great leap and completed the transition from the land to the sea, from the terrestrial existence to a maritime existence.

4

N. The image, which you have shown us, dear Altmann, of the call of the oceans opening themselves, impresses me greatly. And yet, the actual question, the problem of the industrial revolution, still remains unresolved. You ought not to forget, Mr. Altmann, that at that time, in the age of discoveries, a call from the land went out as well. At that time, in the sixteenth and seventeenth centuries, not only the oceans but also the lands and continents opened themselves.

A. Good that you recall this, Mr. Neumeyer. In this dual call from land and sea, the first germ of the contemporary world-dualism between land and sea already expresses itself and the elementary difference between land and sea already shows itself. The English took the ocean; the Russians took from Moscow out to Siberia and completed a purely terrestrial expansion. But how remarkable: on the basis of this gigantic Russian land appropriation, no industrial revolution emerged. The industrial revolution emerged on the island England, an island, the historical situation of which became incomparable because it had taken the step toward maritime existence.

N. That I find simply fanciful! Why couldn't the industrial revolution just as well have emerged upon the continent?

A. Your "couldn't" and your "just as well," I find far more fanciful. In any event, there are humans and even renowned historians who wish to say to one quite precisely what would have happened if, for example, Fredrick the Great had married the Empress Maria Theresa, or if Napoleon had won the Battle of Waterloo, or if the winter of 1941 had not been so terribly cold, and so on. Such unreal propositions appear to me fanciful.

The great events are unique, irrevocable and irretrievable. An historical truth is true only once.[18]

N. Why, then, couldn't an industrial revolution have emerged everywhere?

A. We are speaking concretely of the industrial revolution that is our contemporary fate. It could not emerge anywhere other than in the England of the eighteenth century. An industrial revolution means the unleashing of technological progress, and the unleashing of technological progress is only comprehensible from out of a maritime existence; within a maritime existence it is even sensible up to a certain degree. Technological inventions are made everywhere and at all times. Nor was the technological talent of the English greater than that of other peoples. All that matters is what is made out of the technological inventions, and that depends on the frame, that is to say: in which concrete order the technological invention falls into. Within a maritime existence technological discoveries are developed more freely and with fewer restraints than when they fall into the fixed order of a terrestrial existence and in which they are grasped and bounded. The Chinese invented gunpowder; they were in no way dumber than the Europeans, who also invented it. But in the fixed space of the purely terrestrial order of the China of that time, the invention of gunpowder led only to its use for play and fireworks. In Europe, it led to the inventions of Alfred Nobel and his successors. The English, who in the eighteenth century made all those inventions that led to the industrial revolution – the coal furnace, cast-iron steel, the steam-engine, the spinning jenny, etc. – were in no way more ingenious than the humans of other times and of other lands that remained terrestrial, some of whom had already made the discoveries of the eighteenth century. Technological discoveries are not revelations of a secretive higher spirit. They fall into their own time. They go under or they develop, according to the concrete human complete existence, into which they fall. I want to say this: the discoveries, with which the industrial revolution sets in, could only lead to the onset of an industrial revolution where the step toward a maritime existence had been taken.

N. In the case of England that seems clear to me. But I still don't see the general necessity of this relation between unencumbered technology and maritime existence.

A. Here you touch upon an immense theme. Today, I must satisfy myself by saying to you the following: the midpoint and core of a terrestrial existence – with all its concrete orders – is the house. House and property, marriage, family and hereditary right, all that is built upon the foundation of a terrestrial mode of being [*eines terranen Daseins*], in particular that of the agricultural farm. The farmer, too, as we call him, takes his name not from the work of farming or from tilling the field. The farmer is named after the farm, which is to say the farm house, which belongs to him and to which he belongs. Thus, at the core of a terrestrial existence there stands the house. On the contrary, at the core of a maritime existence there sails the ship, which is already in itself much more and much more intensely a technological means than the house. The house is rest, the ship is movement. Even the space in which the ship moves is other than the space of the landscape, in which the house stands. In consequence, the ship has another environment and another horizon; the humans on the ship have a different kind of social relations both to one another as well as to their external world. They have an essentially different stance toward nature and above all to animals. The terrestrial human tames and domesticates animals: elephants, camels, horses, hounds, cats, oxen, donkeys and all that is his. Fish, on the contrary, are not tamed but only consumed.

N. You are ripping open an abyss, honorable Mr. Altmann.

A. Please pardon me. I allowed myself to get carried away and to name several examples out of the abysmal fullness of the differences between terrestrial and maritime existence. We wished only to clarify to ourselves why the industrial revolution with its unencumbered technology corresponds to a maritime existence. The terrestrial order, in whose center stands the house, necessarily has a fundamentally different relation to technology than a mode of existence, in whose center a ship sails. An absolutization of technology and of technological progress, the equivalence between technological progress and advancement as such, briefly, all that which allows itself to be brought together in the phrase "unencumbered technology," develops only under the presupposition, only on the breeding ground and in the climate of a maritime existence. In following the call of the world oceans opening themselves and in completing the step toward a maritime existence, the island England gave a grand historical answer to the historical call of the age of discoveries. Simultaneously, however, it created the presupposition of the industrial revolution and the beginning of the epoch whose problematic we experience today.

N. I believe I understand what you mean and what the specific particularity of a maritime existence means for your notion of the industrial revolution. Have I understood you correctly if I were to link your construction of an historical call with Arnold Toynbee's[19] method of the challenge?[20] Toynbee describes over twenty different civilizations or cultures through the way that they have responded to a provocation, or to a challenge,[21] as he calls it, which issues out of the particular historical situation and to which the different cultures have given particular answers.

A. That's strikingly apt, Mr. Neumeyer. Actually, I did nothing other than take Toynbee by his word, or rather: I took him by his method. But I remain concrete and do not ask after all possible cultures and epochs. My question is directed to only one concrete question, the answering of which historically clarifies our contemporary epoch of the industrial revolution. This is the question concerning the call, or, if you wish – the challenge,[22] of the industrial revolution. This question I find more important and more exciting than all questions concerning earlier calls of earlier epochs, like the question to which challenge[23] Egyptian culture answered with the pyramids or one of the other more than twenty cultures that Toynbee describes. In addition, I'll give you a clear, concrete answer to our great question concerning the question: the industrial revolution is the logical second stage of a transition toward maritime existence, and this transition toward maritime existence was the great historical answer of the island England to the question or the provocation or the challenge[24] – as you wish – of the world oceans opening themselves.

N. How, then, does Toynbee himself interpret the industrial revolution and unencumbered technology? He, as an Englishman and historian, must actually know it best. This question must actually have been closer to him than the question concerning the challenge[25] of the Egyptians or of the Hittites and Aztecs.

A. Listen to what Toynbee literally says: "Modern technology," he says, "is a splinter that detached itself from our culture around the end of the seventeenth century."[26] You've heard it: a detached splinter! But, in reality, technology did not detach itself, and least of all did it do so as a splinter. In reality, an entire island detached itself from the mainland and took the step toward maritime existence; from this there then followed the industrial revolution and the removal of impediments to technological progress. With this, I have given you the answer to the question concerning the great question and have told you what the industrial revolution answers: it answers to the call or the challenge[27] that was raised in the seventeenth century; it is one part of the answer that England gave to the call of the world oceans as these opened themselves to the humans in the age of discoveries.

5

F. That's grand, what you say here, honorable Mr. Altmann! It is exactly the same as what I say. We are entirely of the same opinion. You see, at that time, during the age of the great discoveries, daring humans ventured forth and found a new world. Today we stand within an age of discoveries much greater than that of four hundred years ago. We are likewise venturing forth, but in correspondingly greater spaces and with correspondingly grander means. At that time, the ocean of the earth opened itself; those spaces were grand, but they were still spaces bound to our little planet, those were earthly spaces. Today, the infinite spaces of the whole cosmos open themselves to us.

A. Would this be the call, so to speak, of the whole cosmos, which today goes out to us?

F. Precisely! On that there's no possible doubt. As I see it, the true age of discoveries has only just now begun. Today, how much more powerful is the call or the challenge[28] or whatever you called it! How small the spaces were at that time, in the age of the so-called discoveries! How great, by contrast, are the spaces that today open themselves to us, be they in the stratosphere or be they beyond the stratosphere in the universe.

A. My dear MacFuture, you speak of a call or challenge[29] of cosmic spaces. How, then, do the cosmic spaces beyond the earth open themselves in an analogous way to the way in which the world oceans upon this earth opened themselves to the humans four hundred years ago? Where is the call or the challenge[30] from the cosmos? I only hear and see that with the means and methods of unencumbered technology you despairingly knock at the spaces of the cosmos and seek with all your power to penetrate into them. But I hear and see nothing of a call or a provocation, with the exception, at best, of flying saucers.

F. Now you ought to allow, Mr. Altmann, that whether you personally hear the call is not the decisive factor. Even then, four hundred years ago, most people didn't notice much. And above all: even then, those who were discovered were not asked in advance. Neither Columbus nor Cortez nor Pizarro nor any other discoverer pleaded with the Aztecs in Mexico or the Incas in Peru or any other Indians for their consent. Neither Columbus nor any other discoverer traveled to the New World with an Indian visa. Discoveries are always made without the visa of the discovered. And you ought to reflect on yet another possibility, good Mr. Altmann: Columbus believed that he was traveling to India and discovered America, a wholly new continent, the existence of which neither Columbus himself nor anyone else had the slightest notion before. Thus, we shall perhaps discover now a fully new planetary body on the way to the moon or to Mars, that nobody had the slightest notion of before. There are more things in heaven and earth than all historians and even all the Nobel Prize winners taken together allow themselves to dream.[31]

A. Here I gladly believe you. But it becomes ever clearer to me, dear MacFuture, that you conceive of your breach into the cosmos as an amplified and intensified new edition of the discovery of America.

F. Perhaps you find that false? Is that not precisely a proof that I am in the right? You, honorable Mr. Altmann, with your historical sense, must actually understand that best.

A. My historical sense keeps me from falling for repetitions. You see, MacFuture, as we Germans entered into the First World War in 1914, we believed that things had to go as they had gone in 1870/1871, as they had in our last victory. As the beleaguered Frenchmen made a sally out of Paris in the winter of 1870/1871, they believed that things had to go as they had gone in the great revolution of 1792. As the American Secretary of State Stimson[32] announced his famed Stimson Doctrine in the year 1932, he believed that things had to go as they had gone in 1861 at the beginning of the war of secession. The human has an almost irresistible need to eternalize his last great historical experience. Precisely my historical sense keeps me from such reprises. My historical sense proves itself above all in that it reminds me of the irretrievable uniqueness of all great historical occurrences. An historical truth is only true *once*. But also the historical call, the challenge[33] that introduces a new epoch is only true *once*. It follows, too that the historical answer that is given to a unique call is only true *once* and only right *once*. It is not always easy to heed this, MacFuture. The impress of the epoch, which proceeds from the historical call and the right answer, is all-too-strong. And above all: the victor won't easily grasp that even his victory is only true *once*.[34]

F. With this, perhaps, you wish to say that I'm providing an old answer to a new historical call?

A. I wish to say precisely that, dear MacFuture. With your breach into the cosmos you give an old answer. Today's call is no longer identical to that of the age in which the oceans opened. Therefore, the answer that was given then is no longer right for today's situation. In addition, all continuations and exacerbations of this erstwhile answer go awry and are useless. You could drive the unencumbered technology into the cosmos ever so desperately, for all I care, you could attempt to make a space ship out of our earth, out of the planet on which we live, on which you can voyage through the cosmos. None of this will do you any good faced with the reality of a new historical call.

F. Then tell us, honorable Mr. Altmann, what the new call is and what we have to do now!

N. Dear MacFuture, with your question concerning the call, you yourself are posing the question concerning the great question. But you shouldn't ask that of our good Mr. Altmann. Mr. Altmann is an historian, and how shall an historian know something of the future? His visage is turned backward. In the best case, he knows when an epoch is at its end – like the famed owl of Minerva.

A. Don't worry about me, gentlemen, I find that it is a gain already if we don't reply to new questions with old answers. We have already achieved much if we don't construe today's new world with the schema of yesterday's new world. I personally don't expect the new call from beyond the stratosphere. As I see it, unencumbered technology encloses the humans more than it opens new spaces to them. Modern technology is useful and necessary. But today it is far from still being the answer to a call. Modern technology satisfies ever new needs, partially those provoked by technology itself. In general, it is itself placed in question, and, therefore, it is no answer. You said earlier, MacFuture, that modern technology has made our earth laughably small. The new spaces, out of which the new call comes, must therefore be found *upon* our earth and not outside in the cosmos. The one who manages to restrain the unencumbered technology, to bind it and to lead it into a concrete order has given more of an answer to the contemporary call than the one who, by means of modern technology seeks to land on the moon or on Mars. The binding of the unencumbered technology – that, for example, would be the labor of a new Hercules. It is from this direction that I hear the new call, the challenge[35] of the present.

N. Dear MacFuture, I, too, find that we don't need to fly to the moon or to Mars. Thanks to modern technology today there opens on our own planet itself enough space without the need for us to immediately push into the cosmos. Above all, the immeasurable depths of the sea open themselves to us. The sea covers over three-fourths of the globe. Up until now one only thought of the surfaces [*Flächen*], that is to say, of the upper surfaces [*Oberflächen*] of the sea. But in the last two decades on the bottom and in the depths of the sea a whole new world has unexpectedly become accessible to us, with unthought-of new life forms and inexhaustible riches. I hear the new call from out of the depths of the sea.

F. Pardon me, gentlemen, but I find you both, both our honorable Mr. Altmann with his new order, but you, too, dear Mr. Neumeyer, with your call from out of the depths of the sea – I find you both not grand enough and much too modest. Fundamentally, for me, this no longer concerns the *call*[36] at all. We have enough *drive*,[37] that's more important, we even have an excess of drive. Thus, I would rather journey to the moon and to Mars than remain on this puny planet.

N. Well then, dear MacFuture, nothing remains for us other than to wish you happy trails.

F. And *I* wish you,[38] dear Mr. Neumeyer, a happy and successful dip into the deep sea. But what then could we both wish for our honorable Mr. Altmann?

A. Many thanks, gentlemen. To me, you need wish nothing new. You shall both have noted that I remain *with* the earth and *upon* the earth.[39] For me, the human is a son of the earth, and so he shall remain as long as he remains human. I would like to hope that both of you shall remain human as well; you, MacFuture, on the moon and on Mars; and you, dear Mr. Neumeyer, in the depths of the sea. But perhaps I may say to you in parting how our common situation on our contemporary earth, our earth threatened by unencumbered technology, appears to me. Surely you know how the second part of Goethe's *Faust* begins: Faust awakes out of a night full of terrible dreams and senses the happiness of a new dawn on earth, which lends him solace and strength, a new beginning. Thus he greets the new world, which now opens itself to him, in the exquisite verse:

You, Earth, stood firm this night.[40]

Just so, I believe that the human shall awake one morning after a hard night threatened by atom bombs and similar terrors and shall gratefully recognize himself again as the son of the firmly grounded earth.[41]

OVERVIEW OF THE TRAJECTORY OF THE DIALOGUE[42]

Notes

Editors' Notes to the Introduction

1 We are grateful to John Thompson of Polity for his enthusiastic response to our idea of publishing these two dialogues in English. We also would like to thank for their help and for sharing their thoughts on the *Dialogues* by Schmitt: Tim Muller from the Hamburg Institute of Social Research, Enzo Traverso from Cornell University and Andrew Arato and Luis Herran Avila from The New School for Social Research.

2 See Gerd Giesler, "Posfacio" in Carl Schmitt, *Diálogo sobre el poder y el acceso al poderoso* (Buenos Aires: Fondo de Cultura Económica, 2010), pp. 93–4.

3 Carl Schmitt, *Diálogos; Diálogo de los nuevos espacios; Diálogo sobre el poder y el acceso al poderoso*, trans. Anima Schmitt de Otero (Madrid: Instituto de Estudios Políticos, 1962).

4 The German edition lacks the Spanish introduction. See Carl Schmitt, *Gespräche. Gespräch über die Macht und den Zugang zum Machthaber, Gespräch über den Neuen Raum*, ed. Gerd Giesler (Berlin: Akademie Verlag, 1994).

5 See the *Dialogue on Power*, p. 25.

6 Schmitt referred to his house as San Casciano, the place where Machiavelli lived after losing favor with the Medici family. See Carlo Galli, *La mirada de Jano. Ensayos sobre Carl Schmitt* (Buenos Aires: Fondo de Cultura Economica, 2011), p. 114.

7 Carl Schmitt, "Historiographia in Nuce: Alexis de

Tocqueville," *Revista de estudios políticos*, 43 (1949): 109–16. This text was also published as part of the book, *Ex captivitate salus* (Cologne: Greven Verlag, 1950), pp. 25–34. See also, Gopal Balakrishnan, *The Enemy: An Intellectual Portrait of Carl Schmitt* (London: Verso, 2002), pp. 256–7.

8 See José Antonio López García, "La presencia de *Carl Schmitt en España*" *Revista de Estudios Políticos*, 91 (1996).

9 General Perón however was not as enthusiastic as some of his Argentine followers, many of them being Argentine fascists turned into Peronists and admirers of Schmitt. In fact, Perón was reticent to offer Schmitt a position because "we are already too much accused of being Nazis to bring here this German Professor." As noted by Jorge Dotti, the influence of Schmitt in Argentina was extensive and his works were even intensively debated during the Argentine constitutional convention of 1949. See Jorge Eugenio Dotti, *Carl Schmitt en Argentina* (Rosario: Homo Sapiens Ediciones, 2000), pp. 110, 121–4 and Reinhard Mehring, *Carl Schmitt: A Biography* (Cambridge: Polity, 2014), p. 454. On Schmitt and constitutional politics, see Andrew Arato's incisive reading, "Multi-Track Constitutionalism Beyond Carl Schmitt," *Constellations*, 18: 3 (2011): 324–51.

10 See Reinhard Mehring, *Carl Schmitt*, pp 421 and also 427, 428, 438, 449 and 471. Also see Carl Schmitt, *Glossarium* (Milan: *Giuffrè*, 2001), entry 25.9.47, p. 25.

11 Carl Schmitt, "Im Vorraum der Macht," *Die Zeit*, 30, July 29, 1954. See also Reinhard Mehring, *Carl Schmitt*, 461 and Gerd Giesler, "Posfacio," pp. 91–2.

12 See Schmitt, Prologue to Spanish Edition, p. 20.

13 Prologue to Spanish Edition, p. 20.

14 Prologue to Spanish Edition, p. 20 in the Zeitlin translation below.

15 Prologue to Spanish Edition, p. 20.

16 In the prologue to the Spanish Edition and not in the dialogue itself.

17 For an insightful critique of Schmitt's normative and humanist 'turn', see Richard Bernstein, "The Aporias of Carl Schmitt," *Constellations*, 18:3 (2011): 403–30. For Freud and the

mythical, see Federico Finchelstein, *El mito del fascismo: de Freud a Borges* (Buenos Aires: Capital intelectual, 2015).

18 Schmitt, *Dialogue on Power*, p. 25; Carl Schmitt, *Political Theology; Four Chapters on the Concept of Sovereignty* (Chicago: University of Chicago Press, 2005).

19 Schmitt, Prologue to Spanish edition, p. 20.

20 For an earlier discussion of the "antechamber of power," see Carl Schmitt, *The Crisis of Parliamentary Democracy* (Cambridge, MA: MIT Press, 1988). Also see, David Ragazzoni, "Carl Schmitt and Global (Dis) Order at the twilight of the Jus Publicum Europaeum," *Journal of Intellectual History and Political Thought*, 2 (2013): 174–9.

21 On Schmitt and the question of technology, see Schmitt, "The Age of Neutralizations and Depoliticizations," *Telos*, 26:2 (1993): 130–42 and John P. McCormick, *Carl Schmitt's Critique of Liberalism: Against Politics as Technology* (Cambridge: Cambridge University Press, 1999).

22 For the *Dialogue on Power*, Schmitt first considered having a real dialogical exchange with the French scholar Raymond Aron and with several others but none of this came to fruition and he then wrote the script of a dialogue between an imaginary other (an exponent of moralist thinking) and himself as the expression of a dialectical mind. See Reinhard Mehring, *Carl Schmitt*, pp. 451, 463–5 and also Gerd Giesler, "Posfacio", pp. 79–80.

23 Carl Schmitt had indeed been a powerful man. He had been a member of the late Weimar antechamber of power and was briefly endowed with a prestigious role in Nazi legal circles. On Schmitt Weimar's and Nazi years, see among others, Joseph W. Bendersky, *Carl Schmitt: Theorist for the Reich* (Princeton: Princeton University Press, 1983); Ellen Kennedy, *Constitutional Failure: Carl Schmitt in Weimar* (Durham, NC: Duke University Press, 2004); Reinhard Mehring, *Carl Schmitt: A Biography*. See also on Schmitt among others, Jan-Werner Müller, *A Dangerous Mind; Carl Schmitt in Post-War European Thought* (New Haven and London: Yale University Press, 2003); Enzo Traverso, *A feu et à sang. De la guerre civile*

européenne 1914–1945 (Paris: Stock, 2007) 282–93; Andreas Kalyvas, *Democracy and the Politics of the Extraordinary: Max Weber, Carl Schmitt, Hannah Arendt,* (Cambridge: Cambridge University Press, 2008).

24 See *Carl Schmitt-Antworten in Nürnberg,* ed. Helmut Quaritsch (Berlin: Duncker & Humblot, 2000), pp. 51, 57, 63, 66. See English translations in *Telos,* 72 (1987): 91–129 and *Telos,* 139 (2007): 35–43. See also Reinhard Mehring, *Carl Schmitt,* p. 41; Gerd Giesler, "Posfacio," pp. 78–9; Joseph W. Bendersky, "Carl Schmitt's Path to Nuremberg: A Sixty-Year Reassessment," *Telos,* 139 (2007): 6–34.

25 Schmitt, *Dialogue on New Space,* p. 52.

26 Carlo Galli, "Carl Schmitt and the Global Age," *The New Centennial Review* 10: 2 (2010): 1–25.

27 See Carl Schmitt, *The Nomos of the Earth in the International Law of the Ius Publicum Europaeum* (New York: Telos Press, 2003); *Hamlet or Hecuba: The Intrusion of the Time into the Play* (New York: Telos Press, 2009); *Theory of the Partisan. Intermediate Commentary on the Concept of the Political* (New York: Telos Press, 2007); Carl Schmitt, *Writings on War,* ed. Timothy Nunan (Cambridge, UK: Polity, 2011); *Spatiality, Sovereignty and Carl Schmitt: Geographies of the Nomos,* ed. Stephen Legg (New York: Routledge, 2011), pp. 25–54.

28 Carl Schmitt, *Land und Meer* (Stuttgart: Klette-Cotta, 1954), pp. 51–7; Roland Axtmann, "Humanity or Enmity? Carl Schmitt on International Politics," *International Politics,* 44 (2007): 531–51.

29 Louiza Odysseos and Fabio Petito (eds.), *The International Political thought of Carl Schmitt: Terror, Liberal War and the Crisis of Global Order* (New York: Routledge, 2007); William Rasch, "A Just War? Or Just a War?: Schmitt, Habermas, and the Cosmopolitan Orthodoxy," *Cardozo Law Review,* 21:5–6 (2000): 1665–85.

30 Jean-François Kervégan, "Carl Schmitt and 'World Unity'," *The Challenge of Carl Schmitt,* ed. Chantal Mouffe (London: Verso, 1999), pp. 54–75.

31 This was not the first time that Schmitt had participated in

radio programs. He had frequently participated in radio shows before 1945. In 1933, he gave a significant interview to German radio. After 1945 he participated in a conversation with Walter Warnach that was broadcasted in Germany in 1951 and also wrote a text on the *Nomos* for another show. See *Un giurista davanti a se stesso. Saggi e interviste* ed. Giorgio Agamben (Vicenza: Neri Pozzi Editore, 2012), pp. 33–9; Reinhard Mehring, *Carl Schmitt*, pp. 451, 463–5 and also Gerd Giesler, "Posfacio", pp. 79–80.

Translator's Notes

Prologue to the 1962 Spanish Edition

1 In 1962 the Institute of Political Studies in Madrid (Instituto de Estudios Politicos) published a translation of Schmitt's *Dialogues* under the title *Diálogos* in a translation by Schmitt's daughter and only child, Anima Schmitt de Otero. The work appeared in the series "Colección Civitas" under the direction of Joaquin Ruiz Gimenez. This translation marked the only time in which both dialogues were published jointly during Schmitt's lifetime, and the work formed a comparison text for Gerd Giesler's 1994 German-language edition of the *Dialogues*, which incorporated changes present in the 1962 Spanish translation, to which Schmitt wrote a "Prologue" (*Prólogo*), which he dated to August, 1961. Cf. Carl Schmitt, *Diálogos; Diálogo de los nuevos espacios; Diálogo sobre el poder y el acceso al poderoso*, trans. Anima Schmitt de Otero (Madrid: Instituto de Estudios Politicos, 1962). There are no notes to Schmitt's 1962 Prologue to the Spanish edition—all notes are those of the translator.

2 This paragraph was omitted from Günter Maschke's 1996 German translation of the *Prólogo*, published in *Schmittiana* V. Cf. Carl Schmitt, *Diálogos*, p. 10 with Carl Schmitt, "Prolog zu „Diálogos" (Madrid 1962)," p. 22 in *Schmittiana, Beiträge zu Leben und Werk Carl Schmitts*, Band V, ed. Piet Tommissen (Berlin: Duncker & Humblot, 1996).

3 In the 1962 Spanish translation, but not in Giesler's 1994 German edition, the *Dialogue on New Space* preceded the *Dialogue on Power and Access to the Holder of Power.*

4 Schmitt's "proseguir," here rendered as "further pursue," could also be rendered as "prosecute."

5 In the 1962 Spanish translation, but not in Giesler's 1994 German edition, the *Dialogue on New Space* preceded the *Dialogue on Power and Access to the Holder of Power.* The "second dialogue" thus here refers to the *Dialogue on Power and Access to the Holder of Power.*

6 Schmitt may appear here to be picking up on the *double entendre* of "*demoníaco,*" which Maschke rendered in his 1996 German translation as "dämonisch." Schmitt might here be distancing himself both from the *daimon* of Socrates as well as the characterization of power that Marx attributes to mechanized factories in chapter 15 of volume I of *Das Kapital.* Cf. Carl Schmitt, "Prolog zu „Diálogos" (Madrid 1962)," p. 22 in *Schmittiana, Beiträge zu Leben und Werk Carl Schmitts,* Band V, ed. Piet Tommissen (Berlin: Duncker & Humblot, 1996).

7 This sentence is omitted in Maschke's German translation of the *Prólogo.* Cf. Carl Schmitt, "Prolog zu „Diálogos" (Madrid 1962)," p. 22 in *Schmittiana, Beiträge zu Leben und Werk Carl Schmitts,* Band V, ed. Piet Tommissen (Berlin: Duncker & Humblot, 1996).

Notes to the Dialogue on Power and Access to
the Holder of Power

1 There are no authorial footnotes in the 1954, 1994, or 2008 German-language editions of Schmitt's *Dialogue on Power and Access to the Holder of Power.* All notes herein are the notes of the translator.

2 Schmitt's epigraph appears to be a reference to Act I, Scene I, lines 121–2 of Lord Byron's play *Cain,* first published in 1821, excerpted from the following dialogic exchange between Byron's characters "Cain" and "Lucifer":

<pre>
LUCIFER   Thou livest and must live forever. Think not
          The earth, which is thine outward cov'ring, is
          Existence; it will cease, and thou wilt be
          No less than thou art now.
CAIN   No less! and why
          No more?
LUCIFER   It may be thou shalt be as we.
CAIN   And ye?
LUCIFER   Are everlasting.
CAIN   Are ye happy?
LUCIFER   We are mighty.
CAIN   Are ye happy?
LUCIFER   No. Art thou?
CAIN   How should I be so? Look on me!
LUCIFER   Poor clay!
          And thou pretendest to be wretched! Thou!
CAIN   I am. And thou, with all thy might, what art thou?
LUCIFER   One who aspired to be what made thee, and
          Would not have made thee what thou art.
CAIN   Ah!
          Thou look'st almost a god; and –
LUCIFER   I am none,
          And having failed to be one, would be nought
          Save what I am. He conquered; let him reign!
</pre>

Lord Byron, *Cain*, Act I, Scene I, lines 116–30. Cf. *Lord Byron's* Cain. *Twelve Essays and a Text with Variants and Annotations*, ed. Truman Guy Stefan (Austin and London: University of Texas Press, 1968), pp. 166–7. In the epigraph, Schmitt introduces an exclamation ("We are mighty!") absent in all English editions of Byron's play. In addition, in attributing the quotation to Byron, Schmitt has omitted the names of the characters associated with the respective utterances.

3   In the 1954 German edition, "*Lord Byron*" is italicized; in the 2008 German edition, "LORD BYRON" is in small capitals; in the 1994 German edition, "Lord Byron" is neither italicized

nor in small capitals. Schmitt (1954), p. [5]; Schmitt (1994), p. [9]; Schmitt (2008), p. [5].

4 In the 1962 Spanish edition of the *Dialogues*, for which Carl Schmitt wrote a prologue and which was translated by his daughter and only child Anima Schmitt de Otero, the "young youth" (*junger Jahrgang*) is presented as a "student" (*Estudiante*), omitting an article or gender marker. Carl Schmitt, *Diálogos. Diálogo de los nuevos espacios. – Diálogo sobre el poder y el acceso al poderoso*, trans. Anima Schmitt de Otero (Madrid: Instituto de Estudios Politicos, 1962), p. 62. In a letter dated 23 January, 1955, Carl Schmitt wrote to Ernst Jünger, "I would still like to experience presenting to you and your wife the private audio recording I possess of the *Dialogue on Power*, on which you wrote me such a substantial letter. It is a dialogue between Anima and me" [*ich möchte es noch erleben, daß ich Ihnen und Ihre Frau das "Gespräch über die Macht", über das Sie mir einen so inhaltreichen Brief geschrieben haben, einmal auf dem privaten Tonband vorführen kann, das ich davon besitze. Es ist ein Gespräch zwischen Anima und mir*]. Carl Schmitt–Ernst Jünger, *Briefe 1930–1983*, ed. Helmut Kiesel (Zweite, ergänzte und überarbeitete Neuausgabe, 2012 [1999]), p. 266.

5 In a letter to Schmitt on reading the published version of the *Dialogue on Power* dated 17 December, 1954, Ernst Jünger wrote, "That you are so wholly without power, as you anticipate on p. 7, neither you nor I believe it." (*Daß Sie so ganz ohne Macht sind, wie Sie auf p. 7 vorwegnehmen, glauben ja weder Sie noch ich.*) Cf. Schmitt (1954), p. 7; Carl Schmitt–Ernst Jünger, *Briefe 1930–1983*, ed. Helmut Kiesel (Zweite, ergänzte und überarbeitete Neuausgabe, 2012 [1999]), p. 263.

6 The term "against" (*gegen*) is italicized in the German original. Cf. Schmitt (1954), p. 7; Schmitt (1994), p. 11; Schmitt (2008), p. 7.

7 The italicization of "*for*" (*für*) is present in the German original. Cf. Schmitt (1954), p. 7; Schmitt (1994), p. 11; Schmitt (2008), p. 7.

8 The italicization of "you" (*Sie*) is present in the German

original. Cf. Schmitt (1954), p. 7; Schmitt (1994), p. 11; Schmitt (2008), p. 8.

9 The reference to a "free-floating intelligentsia" (*freischwebende Intelligenz*) is potentially a reference to Karl Mannheim, *Ideology and Utopia* (*Ideologie und Utopie*) (Bonn: Cohen, 1929), pp. 127–9. This work was published in a third edition in the period preceding the composition of Schmitt's *Dialogues*. Cf. Karl Mannheim, *Ideologie und Utopie* (Frankfurt am Main: Schulte-Bulmke, 1952).

10 Here, Schmitt's character "C.S." may seem to deploy the Marxian idiom of "receding natural limitations" or "receding natural constraints" (*Zurückweichen der Naturschranke*). Marx refers to the receding limitations or constraints of nature in chapter 14 of volume I of *Das Kapital*, the chapter on Absolute and Relative Surplus-Value (*Absoluter und Relativer Mehrwert*), claiming that "In the same measure that industry advances, natural limitations recede." ("Die Gunst der Naturbedingungen liefert immer nur die Möglichkeit, niemals die Wirklichkeit der Mehrarbeit, also des Mehrwerts oder des Mehrprodukts. Die verschiednen Naturbedingungen der Arbeit bewirken, daß dieselbe Quantität Arbeit in verschiednen Ländern verschiedne Bedürfnismassen befriedigt, daß also, unter sonst analogen Umständen, die notwendige Arbeitszeit verschieden ist. Auf die Mehrarbeit wirken sie nur als Naturschranke, d.h. durch die Bestimmung des Punkts, wo die Arbeit für andre beginnen kann. In demselben Maß, worin die Industrie vortritt, weicht diese Naturschranke zurück.") Karl Marx, *Das Kaptial,* vol. I, in *Marx-Engels Werke* (MEW), Band 23, (Berlin/Ost: 1968), p. 537.

11 Schmitt's character "C.S." appears here to refer to the utterances of Nietzsche's characters "Zarathustra" and "the madman" (*der tolle Mensch*), both of whom assert that "God is dead" (*Gott ist tot*). Cf. Friedrich Nietzsche, *Die fröhliche Wissenschaft*, §125; *Also Sprach Zarathustra*, Vorrede §2; Friedrich Nietzsche, *The Gay Science*, trans. Walter Kaufmann (New York: Vintage, 1974), p. 181; Friedrich Nietzsche, *The Portable Nietzsche*, trans. Walter Kaufmann (New York: Penguin, 1976 [1954]), p. 124.

12 According to the editor of the Italian edition of Schmitt's
    Dialogues, Schmitt's character "C.S." appears here to make ref-
    erence to Pierre-Joseph Proudhon's 1846 treatise, *Système des
    contradictions économiques, ou philosophie de le misère.* Cf. P.-J.
    Proudhon, *Système des contradictions économiques, ou philosophie
    de le misère,* in *Œuvres complètes* (Paris : Rivière, 1923–52), 15
    vols., vol. I, pp. 242–53. Cf. Carl Schmitt, *Dialogo sul potere,*
    ed. Giovanni Gurisatti (Milano: Adelphi Edizioni, 2012),
    p. 95 n2.
13 The phrase *"Homo homini lupus"* is given in Latin in the German
    original. Cf. Schmitt (1954), p. 9; Schmitt (1994), p. 13;
    Schmitt (2008), p. 12. Schmitt's character "C.S." appears to cite
    Plautus's play *Asinaria,* Act II, Scene IV, lines 495–96: "Lupus
    est homo homini, non homo, quom qualis sit non novit" (A wolf
    is man to man, not a man, when he does not know what kind [of
    person] he is"). This Latin tag was famously taken up by the phi-
    losopher Thomas Hobbes in the epistle dedicatory to his 1642
    treatise, *De cive,* in which he asserted that "Profecto utrumque
    verè dictum est: *homo homini Deus & homo homini lupus."* ("*There
    are two maxims which are surely both true:* Man is a God to man,
    and Man is a wolf to Man." Cf. Thomas Hobbes, *Elementa phil-
    osophica de cive* (Basel: Flick, 1782), p. vi; Thomas Hobbes, *On
    the Citizen* [*De cive*] (Michael Silverthorne and Richard Tuck
    eds.) (Cambridge: Cambridge University Press, 1998), p. 3.)
14 In her 1962 Spanish translation, Anima Schmitt de Otero
    renders this line as "In Castilian: the human is a wolf to the
    human," deploying her standard equivalent for *der Mensch* to
    translate the Latin term *homo.* Carl Schmitt, *Diálogos. Diálogo
    de los nuevos espacios. – Diálogo sobre el poder y el acceso al poderoso,*
    trans. Anima Schmitt de Otero (Madrid: Instituto de Estudios
    Politicos, 1962), p. 67.
15 The phrase *"Homo homini Deus"* is given in Latin in the German
    original, in which *"Deus"* (God) is capitalized. Cf. Schmitt
    (1954), p. 9; Schmitt (1994), p. 13; Schmitt (2008), p. 12. Like
    the Latin tag *"Homo homini lupus"* ("Man is a wolf to man"),
    the Latin tag *"Homo homini Deus"* ("Man is a God to man")
    was taken up by the philosopher Thomas Hobbes in the epistle

dedicatory to his 1642 treatise, *De cive*, in which he asserted that "Profecto utrumque verè dictum est: *homo homini Deus & homo homini lupus.*" ("*There are two maxims which are surely both true:* Man is a God to man, *and* Man is a wolf to Man." Cf. Thomas Hobbes, *Elementa philosophica de cive* (Basel: Flick, 1782), p. vi; Thomas Hobbes, *On the Citizen* [*De cive*] (Michael Silverthorne and Richard Tuck eds.) (Cambridge: Cambridge University Press, 1998), p. 3.)

16 In her 1962 Spanish translation, Anima Schmitt de Otero renders this line as "In Castilian: the human is a God to the human," deploying her standard equivalent for *der Mensch* to translate the Latin term *homo*. Carl Schmitt, *Diálogos. Diálogo de los nuevos espacios. – Diálogo sobre el poder y el acceso al poderoso*, trans. Anima Schmitt de Otero (Madrid: Instituto de Estudios Politicos, 1962), p. 67.

17 In her 1962 Spanish translation, Anima Schmitt de Otero renders this line as "The human is a human to the human," deploying her standard equivalent for *der Mensch* to translate the Latin term *homo*. Carl Schmitt, *Diálogos. Diálogo de los nuevos espacios. – Diálogo sobre el poder y el acceso al poderoso*, trans. Anima Schmitt de Otero (Madrid: Instituto de Estudios Politicos, 1962), p. 68.

18 In her 1962 Spanish translation, Anima Schmitt de Otero renders this line as "The human is a human to the human," deploying her standard equivalent for *der Mensch* to translate the Latin term *homo*. Carl Schmitt, *Diálogos. Diálogo de los nuevos espacios. – Diálogo sobre el poder y el acceso al poderoso*, trans. Anima Schmitt de Otero (Madrid: Instituto de Estudios Politicos, 1962), p. 68.

19 Alternatively: "something legally reprehensible."

20 Alternatively: "individual legally reprehensible commands."

21 More literally: "What do you wish therewith to say?"

22 Here, Schmitt's character "C.S." appears to refer to the notion of surplus value (*Mehrwert*), which is thematized in Marx's *Das Kapital*.

23 Here, Schmitt's character "C.S." may seem to deploy the Marxian idiom of "receding natural limitations" or "receding

natural constraints" (*Zurückweichen der Naturschranke*). Marx refers to the receding limitations or constraints of nature in chapter fourteen of volume one of *Das Kapital,* the chapter on Absolute and Relative Surplus-Value (*Absoluter und Relativer Mehrwert*), claiming that "In the same measure that industry advances, natural limitations recede." Karl Marx, *Das Kaptial,* vol. I, in *Marx-Engels Werke* (MEW), Band 23, (Berlin/Ost: 1968), p. 537.

24 As noted by Giovanni Gurisatti, the construction of Hobbes's arguments by Schmitt's character "C.S." in this speech in the *Dialogue* may find their closest reference in the third section of chapter one of Hobbes's 1642 treatise *De cive,* a section that has its marginal heading "Humans are by nature equals among themselves" (*Homines naturâ aequales esse inter se*). Cf. Thomas Hobbes, *Elementa philosophica de cive* (Basel: Flick, 1782), I.iii, pp. 8–9; Thomas Hobbes, *On the Citizen* [*De cive*] (Michael Silverthorne and Richard Tuck eds.) (Cambridge: Cambridge University Press, 1998), pp. 25–6; Carl Schmitt, *Dialogo sul potere,* ed. Giovanni Gurisatti (Milano: Adelphi Edizioni, 2012), p. 96n6.

25 Hārūn al-Rashīd (circa 763/766–809) was Caliph of Baghdad from circa 786 until his death. He is a figure in *Les milles et une nuits.*

26 This paragraph is italicized in the 1954 and 1994 German editions of the *Dialogue on Power,* but left unitalicized in the 2008 Klett-Cotta German edition and in the 1962 Spanish translation prepared by Anima Schmitt de Otero. The translation adopts the italicization of the first two German editions (1954 and 1994) in this instance. Cf. Schmitt (1954), p. 18; Schmitt (1962), p. 79; Schmitt (1994), p. 21; Schmitt (2008), p. 28.

27 According to the editor of the Italian edition of the *Dialogues,* this appears to be a reference to the seventh chapter of the third volume of Bismarck's *Thoughts and Reminiscences* (*Gedanken und Erinnerungen*). Cf. Otto von Bismarck, *Gedanken und Erinnerungen,* 3 vols. (Stuttgart/Berlin: Cotta, 1898–1919); Carl Schmitt, *Dialogo sul potere,* ed. Giovanni Gurisatti (Milano: Adelphi Edizioni, 2012), p. 96n7.

28 Heinrich Friedrich Karl vom und zum Stein (1757–1831), Prussian politician considered instrumental in beginning the process of German unification.

29 Friedrich Schiller, *Don Carlos, Infant von Spanien*, Act IV, Scene IV.

30 Friedrich Schiller, *Don Carlos, Infant von Spanien*, Act IV, Scene XXII.

31 The italicization of *"succession"* (*Nachfolge*) is present in the German original. Cf. Schmitt (1954), p. 20; Schmitt (1994), p. 23; Schmitt (2008), p. 32.

32 The italicization of *"I"* (*ich*) is present in the German original. Cf. Schmitt (1954), p. 20; Schmitt (1994), p. 23; Schmitt (2008), p. 33.

33 Alt: "or in any case takes it in claim."

34 Cf. *Romans*, 13:1–13:4.

35 Saint Gregory the Great [Gregorius Magnus] (circa 540–604 CE), Pope Gregory I from 590 CE to 604 CE, wrote dialogues as well as scriptural commentaries.

36 This passage is italicized in the German editions of 1954, 1994, and 2008. Cf. Schmitt (1954), p. 21; Schmitt (1994), p. 24; Schmitt (2008), p. 34. With respect to this passage, Giovanni Gurisatti notes that "The citation by Schmitt is imprecise" ("*La citazione di Schmitt è imprecisa*"). According to Giovanni Gurisatti, Schmitt's quotation is a composite of claims made in Gregory's commentaries on Job and his commentary on the first book of Kings, *Moralia in Job* and *Expositio in librum primum regum*. Carl Schmitt, *Dialogo sul potere*, ed. Giovanni Gurisatti (Milano: Adelphi Edizioni, 2012), p. 97 n12.

37 The italicization of *"will"* (*Wille*) is present in the German original. Cf. Schmitt (1954), p. 21; Schmitt (1994), p. 24; Schmitt (2008), p. 34.

38 The italicization of both phrases "*God is dead*" (*Gott ist tot*) and "*Power in itself is evil*" (*Die Macht ist an sich böse*) is present in the German original. Schmitt (1954), p. 23; Schmitt (1994), p. 26; Schmitt (2008), p. 38.

39 This is potentially a reference to Frederick II of Prussia's

Anti-Machiavell (1740). "C.S." mentions Frederick several times in the *Dialogue*, especially in the third section. Cf. Schmitt (2008 [1954]), p. 22; p. 24.

40 This is potentially a reference to the last line of the second part of Theodor Däubler's 1910 epic poem, *Das Nordlicht*, a poem to which Schmitt devoted his 1916 monograph, *Theodor Däublers "Nordlicht"; Drei Studien über die Elemente, den Geist und die Aktualität des Werkes*. Following her translation of this line in the 1962 Spanish edition of Schmitt's *Dialogues*, Anima Schmitt de Otero gives the only footnote in her translation of the *Dialogue on Power* to provide the German original of this verse. Cf. Theodor Däubler, *Das Nordlicht* (Florentiner Ausgabe) (München und Leipzig: Georg Müller, 1910), 3 vols., vol. II, "Der Entschluß" [The Decision], p. 541; Carl Schmitt, *Theodor Däublers "Nordlicht"; Drei Studien über die Elemente, den Geist und die Aktualität des Werkes* (Dritte Auflage) (Berlin: Duncker & Humblot, 2009 [1916]); Carl Schmitt, *Diálogos. Diálogo de los nuevos espacios. – Diálogo sobre el poder y el acceso al poderoso*, trans. Anima Schmitt de Otero (Madrid: Instituto de Estudios Politicos, 1962), p. 96n1; Carl Schmitt, *Dialogo sul potere*, ed. Giovanni Gurisatti (Milano: Adelphi Edizioni, 2012), p. 98n17.

Dialogue on New Space

1 There are no authorial footnotes in the 1958 or the 1994 German-language editions of Schmitt's *Dialogue on New Space*. All notes herein are the notes of the translator.

2 In the 1962 Spanish edition of Schmitt's *Dialogues* [*Dialogos*] translated by Schmitt's daughter and only child, Anima Schmitt de Otero, with a new preface by Schmitt, a list of dramatis personae precedes the *Dialogue on New Space*, which is absent from the 1958, 1994, and 1995 German-language editions of the *Dialogue on New Space*.
"Protagonistas del Dialogo:
A. – *Altmann* (Viejo historiador).
N. – *Neumeyer* (Físico-químico).

F. – *MacFuture* (Norteamericano)."
Carl Schmitt, *Diálogos; Diálogo de los nuevos espacios; Diálogo sobre el poder y el acceso al poderoso*, trans. Anima Schmitt de Otero (Madrid: Instituto de Estudios Politicos, 1962), p. 15. Anima Schmitt de Otero renders "Partner des Gesprächs" as "Protagonistas del Dialogo" for her translation of the *Dialogue on Power* in the same volume. *ibid.*, p. 62.

3   In the 1958 edition of the *Dialogue on New Space*, a contribution to a Festschrift for the seventieth birthday of Professor Camilo Barcia Trelles of the University of Santiago de Compostela, this sentence continued "upon which our honoured friend Don Camilo has made such fundamental international-legal expositions." [„über den unser verehrter Freund Don Camilo so grundlegende völkerrechtlichen Aus[f]ührungen gemacht hat"] Carl Schmitt, *Gespräch über den Neuen Raum*, in *Estudios de derecho internacional. Homenaje al Profesor Camilo Barcia Trelles* [(eds.) Luis Legaz Lacambra and Luis Garcia Arias] (Santiago de Compostela: Universidad de Santiago de Compostela, 1958), pp. 263–82; p. 263.

This clause was omitted in both the 1962 Spanish edition of Schmitt's *Dialogues* and in the notes to Schmitt's personal copy, found in his papers and *Nachlass*, which served as the basis for Gerd Giesler's 1994 German-language edition. Carl Schmitt, *Diálogos; Diálogo de los nuevos espacios; Diálogo sobre el poder y el acceso al poderoso*, trans. Anima Schmitt de Otero (Madrid: Instituto de Estudios Politicos, 1962), p. 17. Cf. Carl Schmitt, *Gespräche. Gespräch über die Macht und den Zugang zum Machthaber, Gespräch über den Neuen Raum*, ed. Gerd Giesler (Berlin: Akademie Verlag, 1994), p. 37.

4   As noted by the editor of the 1995 German-language edition, see Karl Barth, *Die kirchliche Dogmatik*, III, *Die Lehre von der Schöpfung*, Erster Teil (Zürich: Zollikon, 1945), p 158ff. Carl Schmitt, *Gespräch über den Neuen Raum*, in Carl Schmitt, *Staat, Großraum, Nomos. Arbeiten aus den Jahren 1916–1969*, ed. Günter Maschke (Berlin: Duncker & Humblot, 1995), pp. 552–72, p. 569 n2. This reference is also given in the 2012 Italian edition of Schmitt's *Dialogues* edited by Giovanni

Gurisatti. Cf. Carl Schmitt, *Dialogo sul potere*, ed. Giovanni Gurisatti (Milano: Adelphi Edizioni, 2012), p. 98 n2.

5 Compare Revelation 21:1. The character Altmann's quotation of Revelation 21:1 follows the text of Martin Luther's 1545 vernacular Bible. The translation has used the text of the same passage from the King James Bible in the text above.

6 Schmitt seems here to refer to Admiral Raoul Castex (1878–1968) and his multi-volume *Théories stratégiques* (1929–1935), which appeared in multiple editions. Volume five of the work, published in 1935, bears the subtitle: *la mer contre la terre*. Cf. *Staat, Großraum, Nomos*, ed. G. Maschke (Berlin: 1995), p. 425 n[14]; p. 570 n[6].

7 Schmitt gives the French title of this work in the German original.

8 Alfred Thayer Mahan (1840–1914) was an American admiral and geostrategist. Schmitt discusses Mahan and his theory of geopolitics in section 19 of *Land und Meer, Eine weltgeschichtliche Betrachtung* (Leipzig: Reclam, 1942), pp. 71–2.

9 Alfred von Tirpitz (1849–1930) was a German admiral and Secretary of State of German Imperial Naval Office from 1897–1916.

10 "[das] Wunder" and "[die] Wunder" (pl.) here and throughout are translated as "wonder" and "wonders," respectively, but might also be translated as "miracle" or "miracles."

11 Sir Halford John Mackinder (1861–1947) was an English geographer at the University of Oxford and was later Director of the London School of Economics.

12 "Hegel" is italicized in all three German editions, as well as in Anima Schmitt de Otero's Spanish translation. Cf. Carl Schmitt, *Gespräche. Gespräch über die Macht und den Zugang zum Machthaber, Gespräch über den Neuen Raum*, ed. Gerd Giesler (Berlin: Akademie Verlag, 1994), p. 46; Carl Schmitt, *Gespräch über den Neuen Raum*, in Carl Schmitt, *Staat, Großraum, Nomos. Arbeiten aus den Jahren 1916–1969*, ed. Günter Maschke (Berlin: Duncker & Humblot, 1995), pp. 552–72; p. 558; Carl Schmitt, *Diálogos. Diálogo de los nuevos espacios. – Diálogo sobre el poder y el acceso al poderoso*, trans.

Anima Schmitt de Otero (Madrid: Instituto de Estudios Politicos, 1962), p. 31.

13 In the 1958 (German) and 1962 (Spanish) editions, this interjection is absent and is present only in the 1994 Akademie Verlag edition based on corrections in Schmitt's hand to his personal copy of the *Dialogue on New Space*. In the other editions, MacFuture's first two speeches are one uninterrupted monologue. Cf. Carl Schmitt, *Gespräche. Gespräch über die Macht und den Zugang zum Machthaber, Gespräch über den Neuen Raum*, ed. Gerd Giesler (Berlin: Akademie Verlag, 1994), p. 46; Carl Schmitt, *Gespräch über den Neuen Raum*, in Carl Schmitt, *Staat, Großraum, Nomos. Arbeiten aus den Jahren 1916–1969*, ed. Günter Maschke (Berlin: Duncker & Humblot, 1995), pp. 552–72; p. 558; Carl Schmitt, *Diálogos. Diálogo de los nuevos espacios. – Diálogo sobre el poder y el acceso al poderoso*, trans. Anima Schmitt de Otero (Madrid: Instituto de Estudios Politicos, 1962), pp. 31–2.

14 In Anima Schmitt de Otero's 1962 Spanish translation, for which Schmitt wrote a prologue, this exclamation ("Gerechter Himmel!"), perhaps more literally rendered as "Just heaven!" or "Heavenly justice!" or "By justice in heaven!" is rendered as "¡Cielo Santo!" ("Holy heaven!"). Carl Schmitt, *Diálogos; Diálogo de los nuevos espacios; Diálogo sobre el poder y el acceso al poderoso*, trans. Anima Schmitt de Otero (Madrid: Instituto de Estudios Politicos, 1962), p. 34.

15 "Island" (*Insel*) is italicized in the German original.

16 Sir John Robert Seeley (1834–95) was an English historian and Regius Professor of Modern History at the University of Cambridge. The library of the History Faculty of the University of Cambridge was and is named in his honor.

17 Schmitt's Altmann seems to be quoting from Seeley's 1883 monograph based on lectures at Cambridge, *The Expansion of England*: "There is something very characteristic in the indifference that we show towards this mighty phenomenon of the diffusion of our race and the expansion of our state. We seem, as it were, to have conquered and peopled half the world in a fit of absence of mind. While we were doing it, that is, in the

eighteenth century, we did not allow it to affect our imaginations or in any degree to change our ways of thinking; nor have we even now ceased to think of ourselves as simply a race inhabiting an island off the northern coast of the Continent of Europe." J. R. Seeley, *The Expansion of England; Two Courses of Lectures* (Cambridge: Cambridge University Press, 2010 [1883]), p. 8. Schmitt's Altmann shifts the quote by removing Seeley's language of appearance. In the version quoted by Schmitt's Altmann, "we seem ... to have conquered" becomes "we conquered" or "we have conquered" (*haben wir die Welt erobert*). In addition, Schmitt's Altmann gives only half of the sentence quoted – where Seeley claimed that the English had "conquered *and peopled half* the world," Schmitt's Altmann both contracts and expands the claim in the quotation – omitting the claim that the English had "peopled" half the world and omitting the "half."

18 Jan-Werner Müller translates this line as "A historical truth is only true once." Cf. Jan-Werner Müller, *A Dangerous Mind; Carl Schmitt in Post-War European Thought* (New Haven: Yale University Press, 2003), p. 104.

19 Arnold J. Toynbee (1889–1975) was a British historian, whose work, *The World and the West* (Oxford: Oxford University Press, 1953), appears to be cited by Schmitt's characters below.

20 Neumeyer's "challenge" is here given in English in the German original.

21 Neumeyer's "challenge" is in English in the German original.

22 Altmann's "challenge" is in English in the German original.

23 Altmann's "challenge" is in English in the German original.

24 Altmann's "challenge" is in English in the German original.

25 Neumeyer's "challenge" is in English in the German original.

26 A variation of this quote appears in Chapter V, "The Psychology of Encounters," of Arnold Toynbee's 1953 monograph, *The World and the West*: "We saw that, on the first occasion, the West tried to induce the Far Eastern peoples to adopt the Western way of life in its entirety, including its religion as well as its technology, and that this attempt did not succeed. And then we saw that, in the second act of the play,

the West offered to the same Far Eastern peoples a secularized excerpt from the Western civilization in which religion had been left out and technology, instead of religion, had been made the central feature; and we observed that this technological splinter, which had been flaked off from the religious core of our civilization towards the end of the seventeenth century, did succeed in pushing its way into the life of a Far Eastern Society that had previously repulsed an attempt to introduce the Western way of life *en bloc* – technology and all, including religion." Cf. Arnold Toynbee, *The World and the West* (New York: Oxford University Press, 1953), p. 67.

27 Altmann's "challenge" is in English in the German original.
28 MacFuture's "challenge" is in English in the German original.
29 Altmann's "challenge" is in English in the German original.
30 Altmann's "challenge" is in English in the German original.
31 This line contains a potential Shakespearean allusion and paraphrase. Cf. Shakespeare, *Hamlet*, I.v ll. 167–8. Schmitt began work on the lectures that became *Hamlet or Hecuba* (1956) in 1955, the year in which the *Dialogue on New Space* was composed and first aired on German radio.
32 Henry L. Stimson (1867–1950) was U.S. Secretary of State from 1929 to 1933 during the administrations of President Herbert Hoover, as well as U.S. Secretary of War in the administrations of Presidents William Howard Taft (in the period 1911–13), Franklin Delano Roosevelt (in the period 1940–5), and Harry Truman (1945).
33 Altmann's "challenge" is English in the original.
34 Throughout this paragraph "once" (*einmal*) is italicized in the 1958, 1994, and 1995 German editions as well as in the 1962 Spanish translation prepared by Anima Schmitt de Otero. Schmitt, *Gespräch über den Neuen Raum* (1958), p. 280; Schmitt, *Diálogos* (1962), p. 54; Schmitt, *Gespräche* (1994), p. 61; Schmitt, *Gespräch über den Neuen Raum* (1995), p. 567.
35 Altmann's "challenge" is English in the German original, although capitalized to accord with German orthography. Carl Schmitt, *Gespräche. Gespräch über die Macht und den Zugang zum Machthaber, Gespräch über den Neuen Raum*, ed.

Gerd Giesler (Berlin: Akademie Verlag, 1994), p. 63; Carl Schmitt, *Gespräch über den Neuen Raum,* in Carl Schmitt, *Staat, Großraum, Nomos. Arbeiten aus den Jahren 1916–1969,* ed. Günter Maschke (Berlin: Duncker & Humblot, 1995), pp. 552–72, p. 568.

36 MacFuture's "call" (*Anruf*) is marked off in italics in the German original.

37 MacFuture's "drive" (*Antrieb*) is marked off in italics in the German original.

38 MacFuture's personal pronoun (*ich*) is marked off in italics in the German original. Carl Schmitt, *Gespräche. Gespräch über die Macht und den Zugang zum Machthaber, Gespräch über den Neuen Raum,* ed. Gerd Giesler (Berlin: Akademie Verlag, 1994), p. 64; Carl Schmitt, *Gespräch über den Neuen Raum,* in Carl Schmitt, *Staat, Großraum, Nomos. Arbeiten aus den Jahren 1916–1969,* ed. Günter Maschke (Berlin: Duncker & Humblot, 1995), pp. 552–72, p. 568.

39 Altmann's emphatic prepositions (*bei . . . auf*) are italicized in the German original. Carl Schmitt, *Gespräche. Gespräch über die Macht und den Zugang zum Machthaber, Gespräch über den Neuen Raum,* ed. Gerd Giesler (Berlin: Akademie Verlag, 1994), p. 64; Carl Schmitt, *Gespräch über den Neuen Raum,* in Carl Schmitt, *Staat, Großraum, Nomos. Arbeiten aus den Jahren 1916–1969,* ed. Günter Maschke (Berlin: Duncker & Humblot, 1995), pp. 552–72, p. 569.

40 Goethe, *Faust II*, Act I, l. 4681.

41 In the 1958 edition of the *Dialogue on New Space*, which was published as a chapter in a Festschrift for Camilo Barcia Trelles, Professor of International Law at the University of Santiago de Compostela, a further sentence followed in Altmann's final monologue: "Let us now ask our honored friend and teacher Don Camilo, who among the three of us is right?" (*Fragen wir jetzt unseren verehrten Freund und Lehrer Don Camilo, wer von uns dreien Recht hat?*). Carl Schmitt, *Gespräch über den Neuen Raum,* in *Estudios de derecho internacional. Homenaje al Profesor Camilo Barcia Trelles* [(eds.) Luis Legaz Lacambra and Luis Garcia Arias] (Santiago de Compostela: Universidad

de Santiago de Compostela, 1958), pp. 263–82; p. 282. This
sentence is omitted from Gerd Giesler's 1994 edition based
on changes made in Carl Schmitt's personal copy of the
Dialogue as well as in the Spanish translation prepared by
Schmitt's daughter, Anima Schmitt de Otero in 1962. Carl
Schmitt, *Diálogos. Diálogo de los nuevos espacios – Diálogo
sobre el poder y el acceso al poderoso*, trans. Anima Schmitt de
Otero (Madrid: Instituto de Estudios Politicos, 1962), p. 58.
The final sentence was restored in the 1995 German edition
published in *Staat, Großraum, Nomos*, which is based on the
1958 text rather than Schmitt's subsequent marginal changes.
Carl Schmitt, *Gespräch über den Neuen Raum*, in Carl Schmitt,
Staat, Großraum, Nomos. Arbeiten aus den Jahren 1916–1969,
ed. Günter Maschke (Berlin: Duncker & Humblot, 1995), pp.
552–72, p. 569.

42 The "Overview of the Trajectory of the Dialogue" ("Übersicht
über den Gang des Gespräches") is absent from the 1958 and
1995 German-language editions and from the 1962 Spanish
edition, translated by Schmitt's daughter, Anima Schmitt de
Otero, but is present in the 1994 German language edition prepared by Gerd Giesler on the basis of material in the Schmitt
Nachlass and Schmitt's personal copy of the 1958 edition. Cf.
Carl Schmitt, *Gespräch über den Neuen Raum*, in *Estudios de
derecho internacional. Homenaje al Profesor Camilo Barcia Trelles*,
eds. Luis Legaz Lacambra and Luis Garcia Arias (Santiago
de Compostela: Universidad de Santiago de Compostela,
1958), pp. 263–82; p. 282; Carl Schmitt, *Diálogos; Diálogo de
los nuevos espacios; Diálogo sobre el poder y el acceso al poderoso*,
trans. Anima Schmitt de Otero (Madrid: Instituto de Estudios
Politicos, 1962), p. 58; Carl Schmitt, *Gespräche. Gespräch über
die Macht und den Zugang zum Machthaber, Gespräch über den
Neuen Raum*, ed. Gerd Giesler (Berlin: Akademie Verlag,
1994), p. 65; Carl Schmitt, *Gespräch über den Neuen Raum*,
in Carl Schmitt, *Staat, Großraum, Nomos. Arbeiten aus den
Jahren 1916–1969*, ed. Günter Maschke (Berlin: Duncker &
Humblot, 1995), pp. 552–72, p. 569.

Works Consulted

Editions of the Dialogues *in German*

Carl Schmitt, *Gespräch über die Macht und den Zugang zum Machthaber* (Pfullingen: Günther Neske Verlag, 1954).

Carl Schmitt, *Gespräch über den Neuen Raum*, in *Estudios de derecho internacional. Homenaje al Profesor Camilo Barcia Trelles*, eds. Luis Legaz Lacambra and Luis Garcia Arias (Santiago de Compostela: Universidad de Santiago de Compostela, 1958), pp. 263–82.

Carl Schmitt, *Gespräche. Gespräch über die Macht und den Zugang zum Machthaber, Gespräch über den Neuen Raum*, ed. Gerd Giesler (Berlin: Akademie Verlag, 1994).

Carl Schmitt, *Gespräch über den Neuen Raum*, in Carl Schmitt, *Staat, Großraum, Nomos. Arbeiten aus den Jahren 1916–1969*, ed. Günter Maschke (Berlin: Duncker & Humblot, 1995), pp. 552–72.

Carl Schmitt, *Gespräch über die Macht und den Zugang zum Machthaber*, ed. Gerd Giesler (Stuttgart: Klett-Cotta, 2008).

Editions of the Dialogues *in Spanish*

Carl Schmitt, *Diálogos. Diálogo de los nuevos espacios – Diálogo sobre el poder y el acceso al poderoso*, trans. Anima Schmitt de Otero (Madrid: Instituto de Estudios Politicos, 1962).

Editions of the Dialogues *in Italian*

Carl Schmitt, *Dialogo sul potere*, ed. Giovanni Gurisatti (Milano:
Adelphi Edizioni, 2012).

Index